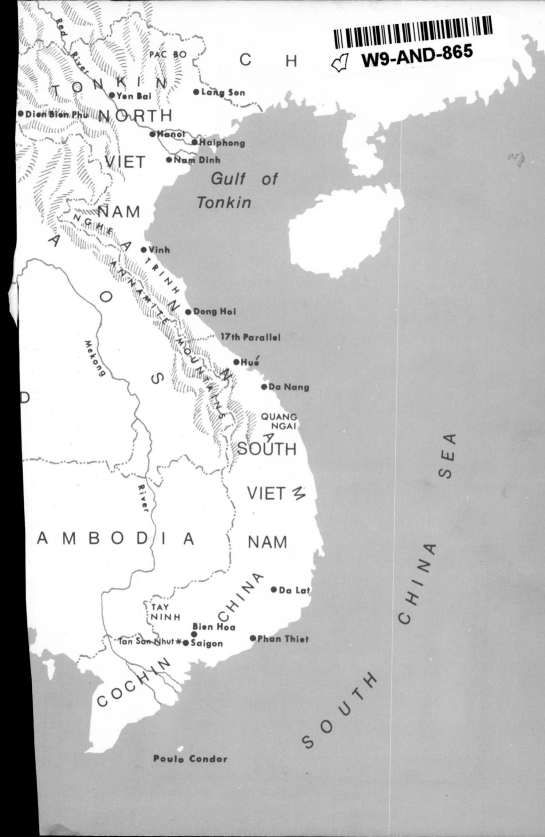

The Vietnamese Revolution

THE
Vietnamese
REVOLUTION

Robert
Goldston

THE BOBBS-MERRILL COMPANY, INC.·

Indianapolis   New York

For Jasmine Moti-Walal
The clash of East and West . . .

THE BOBBS-MERRILL COMPANY, INC.
PUBLISHERS   INDIANAPOLIS   NEW YORK

Text copyright © 1972 by Robert Goldston
Map by Jack H. Fuller
Design by Jack Jaget
Printed in the United States of America
Library of Congress catalog card number: 77–172347
0   9   8   7   6   5   4   3   2   1

Contents

The Vietnamese Revolution

CLOSE-UP

Operation Mastiff

THE EARLY dawn hours of February 21, 1966 (the sky to the east flaming with the suddenness of tropical sunrise), burst over the sleeping rice paddies and the silent green jungles surrounding the Michelin rubber plantation in South Vietnam with the roar of many Niagaras. For on this day, transported in hundreds of helicopters, the fifteen thousand men of the United States First Infantry Division along with elements of the United States First Cavalry Division (Armored) swooped down from the peaceful skies to begin a large search-and-destroy mission known as Operation Mastiff.

From South Vietnamese agents, from aerial reconnaissance, from enemy deserters had come the information, weeks before, that the Michelin rubber plantation and the villages, fields, jungles and hills around it constituted a major base of the insurgent Viet Cong rebels and their North Vietnamese allies. This information, digested by divisional, army and central intelligence staffs, had started in motion the vast and complex machinery of command; from the Joint Chiefs of Staff in Washington's Pentagon to Army Command Headquarters in Saigon to Divisional Headquarters in the town of Lai Khe, plans and orders had gone forth for a massive undertaking that should catch the enemy totally by surprise.

Totally by surprise? Somehow the Viet Cong had known for weeks that the Americans would pounce on the Michelin rubber plantation. In preparation for their arrival the Viet Cong had labored night and day over many thousands of interesting "Welcome!" devices. These included *punji* pits—camouflaged holes into which needle-sharp poisoned bamboo stakes had been implanted; mines that exploded underfoot, mines that exploded by trip-wire, mines that exploded by timing devices and mines that could be exploded electrically from a distance; wooden boards faced with poisoned steel nails and drawn back by bent saplings that would slam into the faces of patrols—and many other ingenious death-to-the-unwary booby traps. Totally by surprise? Well, tactically—yes. For on February 21 it turned out that the orders to seize the Michelin rubber plantation had only been a counter-intelligence fake. The U.S. Army was landing its men, no doubt to the vexation and mortification of the laborious Viet Cong, some miles from the Michelin deathtraps. The plantation was surrounded.

The infantrymen of the First Division were unaware, of course (even their battalion commanders had suspected nothing until a few hours earlier), of the cunning ruse by which the army had spared them the Viet Cong welcome; they had their own problems. Carrying field rations, gas masks, extra ammunition, rifles, recoilless rifles, mortars, machine guns of various caliber, grenades, bayonets, steel helmets, ponchos and even toothpaste and toothbrushes as the "choppers" settled onto the dry rice paddies, they poured sluggishly out, raced a few yards and threw themselves prone—overburdened ants dispersed around giant spiders. Then the spiders lifted away and the infantrymen were on their own. It took them several minutes to realize they were truly alone. The paddies and jungles were devoid of any enemy. Their only foes were innumerable insects, the heat (100° in the shade) and the oppressive silence. Soon sergeants were ordering them to "move out!"

A combined team of First Cavalry and First Infantry—the men walking ahead of fifteen-ton armored personnel carriers (APCs) —approached a straw-thatched Vietnamese village. Here they carried out a "reconnaissance by fire." That is, the machine gunners handling the huge fifty-caliber weapons mounted on the APCs swept the entire village with thousands of rounds of death. The villagers had no doubt already fled, and if any Viet Cong snipers or patrols lurked there they would presumably return fire. But the village was deserted. As the combat team pushed on, the infantrymen set fire to all its buildings. Back at Divisional Headquarters the commanding general had ordered: "No houses are to be burned unless they contain Viet Cong snipers." This order had been understood by battalion commanders to be: "Houses containing Viet Cong snipers are to be burned." Company commanders told their lieutenants: "If you burn any houses you better be sure there are Viet Cong in them!" The lieutenants told

Into the Michelin plantation, its rubber tree jungle concealing only fear.

the sergeants: "You can burn any houses with Viet Cong in
them." The sergeants told the men: "Better burn those houses—
probably Viet Cong in them."

Company B of the First Battalion of the First Infantry Division, as it threaded its way warily through the jungle, came upon
several large stores of rice. This rice—the staple food of Vietnam
—could have been either a Viet Cong supply dump or the storage
area of local villagers. A South Vietnamese Army lieutenant, on
liaison with Company B, after inspecting the rice, cheerfully
announced that it was undoubtedly Viet Cong. The rice was
burned. During the following five days of Operation Mastiff, all
food supplies uncovered in the area and almost all villages would
be burned.

On the fourth day of Operation Mastiff, as C Company of the
Second Battalion was walking cautiously across a rice paddy
toward the nearby wall of jungle, the enemy suddenly made his
presence known—in the shape of a hail of rifle and machine-gun
fire from the jungle's edge. Several of C Company's men were
killed, more wounded in the ambush. The survivors instantly
threw themselves prone and commenced to return fire (though
none of them could see an enemy—they simply shot toward the
deadly trees) while the company commander radioed for air support. Within minutes an air strike came in—F-100 Supersabres
screaming out of the sky, dropping fragmentation and napalm
bombs and spraying the jungle with 20mm. cannon shells and
rockets. As the napalm took hold, soon the entire forest was afire.
What effect this may have had on the enemy, C Company never
learned—no bodies were found, at any rate.

Such close-in air support was far from the only devastation on
which the First Division could rely. Its company commanders
could call up armed-to-the-teeth helicopters that would hover
over suspected enemy concentrations and spray them with
machine-gun and rocket fire. First Division artillery would be directed by slow-flying observation planes; its wounded would be
evacuated by medical helicopters; if necessary, supplies would be
dropped to it from giant cargo planes. Under certain circumstances it could request the air force to send in defoliation planes,
low-flying aircraft adapted to spray wide areas of jungle with vege-

tation-killing poisons. Perhaps the most devastating weapon on call could only be requested by the divisional commander—a special strike by the gigantic B-52 Intercontinental Bombers of the Strategic Air Command based thousands of miles away on the island of Guam. These huge planes, originally built to carry nuclear bombs halfway around the world and then return, could transport a mighty weight of 750- and 1,000-pound bombs. They flew so high (50,000 feet) that they could be neither seen nor heard. The first intimation of their presence would be when the jungle for miles around suddenly erupted in a roaring earthquake of flame.

On the last day of Operation Mastiff, a company of the Third Battalion, being carried through the smoking wreckage of a Vietnamese village in their giant APCs, discovered what it thought to be an enemy bunker. There was a hut—or the wreckage of a hut—aboveground and under this a large cavern dug into the ground. While one of the APCs paused, an infantryman jumped down and rolled a grenade into the "bunker." It exploded, and a crowd of shrieking women and children rushed forth. Behind them they left a seven-year-old girl and her mother, both dead.

Chapter One

THE STARVING SEA HORSE

> There is a legend, in our country as well as in China, on the miraculous "Book of the Wise." When facing great difficulties, one opens it and finds a way out.
>
> —HO CHI MINH

CERTAINLY no nation ever faced greater difficulties, ever required a "Book of the Wise" more than the twenty-four million vivid, imaginative, generous and thoroughly turbulent people crowded between the Annamite Mountains and the South China Sea in the land of Vietnam. With its chaotic history, its mixture of many peoples, cultures and languages, the enervating heat of its equatorial climate, the almost constant wars and rebellions that have disrupted it for many centuries, perhaps the most remarkable fact about Vietnam is that it still exists as an independent state. But to the Vietnamese people, inhabiting a nation shaped like a starving sea horse suspended from the huge belly of China, independence has always been more than a hope, more than a fact—it has been a passion.

A starving sea horse? Yes, because although more than one thousand miles separate its northern and southern extremities, Vietnam is at the most no more than 330 miles wide; at the least (in the center) a bare 40. Its internal geography displays three distinct variations on the same theme—variations that have contributed

to more than one conquest, more than one divisive colonial exploitation. Northern Vietnam is a circle of mountain ranges (the
foothills of great peaks marching north into China and west into
Laos) surrounding the rich delta of the Red River. It is on the
delta of this 745-mile-long river (rising in China) that most of
North Vietnam's population lives, and where stand the cities of
Hanoi (upriver) and Haiphong, a natural harbor on the sea.
Central Vietnam is no more than a long, thin series of little plains
separating the Annamite Mountains from the sea. On the most
important of these little plains stands the city of Hué. Southern
Vietnam is largely the land left behind by the alluvial deposits of
the Mekong River as it has poured for millennia from Laos to the
sea. In the marshy paddies of the Mekong River delta is grown a
truly staggering amount of rice—and on one of the Mekong's
many branches to the sea stands the city of Saigon, largest in
Vietnam.

The climate of Vietnam may be described as unremittingly hot
(a little milder in the north than the south) from October to May
and unceasingly rainy (the heavy monsoons) from May to October. Where there are no villages, cities or rice paddies there are
forests so dense with undergrowths of bamboo as to deserve the
name of jungles. Deer, buffaloes, wild oxen, elephants, tigers and
panthers are to be found abundantly in the mountainous areas to
which they have retreated as human habitation has spread. They
share the mountains with various semicivilized tribes driven there
centuries ago by wars and political upheavals on the lowlands.

There are many towns in Vietnam with more than 20,000 inhabitants; of the large cities, Hué boasts 96,000, Haiphong 170,-
000, Da Lat 250,000, Hanoi 405,000 and Saigon more than
1,800,000. The rest of the population—the vast majority—live
in small villages, each surrounded by a bamboo wall, each con-
stituting a largely self-governing commune presided over by village
elders and notables.

Evidence of human habitation dating back to Neolithic times
has been uncovered in Vietnam; skulls of an Indonesian type have
been found, making these islanders from the south, presumably,
the first to inhabit the land. During the Bronze Age Mongoloid
people from China moved south into Vietnam, mingled with the

18 THE VIETNAMESE REVOLUTION

Indonesians in the rich Red River delta region and produced the
Vietnamese. By turning the marshes of the delta into rice paddies
an ever larger population could be supported. Some, at least, of
the original Indonesian inhabitants did not take kindly to the
Chinese newcomers, however, because they retreated into the
mountains west of the delta—only to be pushed over into Laos
before new waves of Chinese immigrants.

South of the Red River delta, the Indonesians were able to
maintain control. An Indonesian tribe called the Chams built up
a flourishing kingdom there during the Middle Ages. The Chams
were Hindus, having been converted from their older paganism by
missionaries from India about A.D. 200. They were also seafarers—
trading in spices, aloes and ivory up and down the China coast
and south to Malaysia and the Indonesian islands. Their kingdom
of Champa lasted for about 1,200 years but was almost contin-
ually engaged in warfare against neighboring Cambodia—a feud
that permanently weakened both kingdoms.

The Mekong River delta south of the Champa kingdom was
the stronghold of yet another branch of the Indonesian people,
the Khmers, who, although they established their own kingdom,
remained largely under the domination of Cambodia. Hindus and
seafarers like the Chams, the Khmers developed a highly sophisticated civilization that owed much more to Indian than to
Chinese influences.

Both the Chams and the Khmers were eventually to succumb
to the steady expansion of the Vietnamese people pushing south
from the Red River delta; indeed, the history of Vietnam for
almost two thousand years was that of Vietnamese penetration to
the south and Vietnamese resistance to Chinese incursion from
the north.

Official Chinese penetration of Vietnam (as opposed to the
migration of Chinese people south, which had been going on for
centuries) may be said to have commenced in 207 B.C. In that
year a Chinese general who had been appointed governor of the
southernmost province of China decided to set up a kingdom for
himself to the south of the Celestial Empire. After all, the emperor and his court were far away, and the people of the Red River
delta region could offer no real resistance to the general's troops.

The general called this new kingdom he established around the Red River delta "Vietnam," meaning "land-of-the-south."

This kingdom of Vietnam, however, was overthrown in the year 111 B.C. by the vigorous new Han Dynasty that had come to power in China. The old general's private little kingdom was now incorporated into the Chinese Empire as the province of Annam ("dominion-of-the-south"). The Chinese were far from brutal conquerors. Confucius had long ago declared, "Let those who call themselves Chinese be Chinese," meaning that if a subject people would acknowledge the overlordship of the emperor and adopt Chinese ways, then they should be treated as full citizens of the empire. Unfortunately for the Chinese, however, the Vietnamese, while copying willingly everything of value from Chinese culture, would not consider themselves Chinese, nor would they recognize the overlordship of the emperor. Revolts against the Chinese were numerous (one, in A.D. 43, was led by two sisters), but met with no success. Vietnamese obstinance did, however, provoke the Chinese T'ang emperors (successors to the Hans) to rule their rebellious southern province most oppressively. Chinese armies were stationed in Vietnam, taxes were increased, notable Vietnamese were carted off to permanent exile in China and all protest was savagely repressed. T'ang policy was not more successful in stamping out Vietnamese aspirations to independence than had been the more conciliatory policy of the Hans. With the passing of the T'ang Dynasty in China, the Celestial Empire's influence in Vietnam gradually weakened until, by the end of the tenth century, Vietnam was able to regain its independence, although it had to theoretically acknowledge Chinese overlordship.

With the expulsion of the Chinese, Vietnam fell for a while into a period of anarchic feudalism. Local "strongmen," survivors of campaigns against the Chinese or the Chams to the south, established themselves as a sort of brigand nobility throughout the country, carving out small strongholds for themselves and forcing the peasants into the role of serfs. The warfare these strongmen carried on against each other and their heavy oppression of the peasantry soon brought ruin to the land. It was not until the eleventh century that a powerful family, the Li, were able to subdue their rivals and once again unite Vietnam under a single government. The Li Dynasty lasted until the thirteenth century, when it was replaced by the Tran Dynasty. The centuries of relative peace imposed by the Lis had greatly strengthened Vietnam—and the proof of this was the fact that the Trans in the thirteenth century were able to defeat a Mongol army sent by the Mongol emperor of China, Kublai Khan, to regain the lost province. It is worth noting that this is one of the very few occasions in history that any Mongol army was defeated—either in Asia or in Europe.

The Trans were not only able to defend themselves against the Mongols; they also undertook to conquer the Champa kingdom to the south of Vietnam. Continuous border raids, skirmishes and battles merged into a long period of intermittent warfare that saw the Vietnamese inching ever farther south, the power of the Chams ever declining. The Tran policy of southern expansion, with its continuous border warfare, eventually weakened both the country and the dynasty—so much so that early in the fifteenth century the Chinese were once again able to regain actual as well as theoretical control of Vietnam. But after a few years the northern interlopers were once again driven from the country, this time by a new Vietnamese dynasty, the Le. The great Le ruler Le Thanh Ton (1466–1497) undertook a final campaign against the Chams, decisively defeated them in 1470 and incorporated most of the Champa kingdom into Vietnam.

Taking a leaf from their Chinese neighbors' age-old book of conquest, the Vietnamese established military colonies throughout the former Cham territories. Settled by soldiers' families, these were self-sustaining communities devoted to normal domestic enterprises such as rice cultivation or trade. Far from exploiting their Cham neighbors, these new communal villages fit peacefully into the local economy. It was a method of maintaining an army of occupation calculated to create the least possible friction with a conquered people.

From the subdued Cham lands the Vietnamese now moved southward into the territory of the Khmers around the Mekong River delta. The Khmers had already been decimated by their endless wars with their Siamese and Laotian neighbors and by the sixteenth century could offer no effective resistance. By the beginning of the nineteenth century the Vietnamese had overrun the entire Mekong delta region, and after two thousand years of sometimes peaceful, sometimes warlike penetration, they now ruled over the entire area of what we know as Vietnam.

But although Vietnam was now demographically one, it was not really united politically. While the emperors of the Le Dynasty were still theoretically supreme, real power, from the sixteenth century on, had been shared by two families, the Trinh in the north and the Nguyen in the former Cham lands. In fact the Nguyen styled themselves "kings" and maintained a capital at Hué. The expansion of the empire over the Khmer territories had really been the work of the Nguyen family, and as the power of the "kings of Hué" increased, their interests came more and more into conflict with those of the Trinh family to the north, the family that dominated the Le Dynasty emperors.

The insurrection of the Tay Son (1773) overthrew both the Trinh and the Nguyen families' power. But a fifteen-year-old Nguyen survivor, Nguyen Anh, fled to the south. There he organized a counterrevolution, and with the help of a French missionary bishop, Pigneau de Behaine, and various French officers he was able to defeat the Tay Son rebels in a fighting advance to the north. He entered Hanoi in 1802 and, under the name of Gia Long, assumed the title of emperor of all Vietnam as the founder of the Nguyen Dynasty. How Nguyen Anh secured French help—and what that aid was to cost him and his successors—we will consider later. Ironically, the triumph of Nguyen Anh and the establishment of his imperial dynasty over all of Vietnam was to mark not the beginning of new national greatness, but the slow decline of Vietnamese fortunes. But before examining the somber story of the French conquest and colonial exploitation of Vietnam, it may be useful to take a closer look at the social structure and life of the country before it entered the twilight of its independence.

The Vietnamese language may be considered a very much modified branch of Chinese. Until the coming of the French, it was written in pictograph style like the Chinese, each pictograph representing a word, and combinations or parts of pictographs forming derivative words. Also like the Chinese it was an

extremely difficult language in which to become literate. This fact
was of great importance in the social and political development
of the country, for national and even regional governmental administration required literacy, which in turn required many years
of education—years of education far beyond the reach of the
great majority of poor Vietnamese peasants. Since only the rich
could afford the education necessary to administer the country,
only the rich ruled. Kings and emperors might come and go,
but what we would today call the bureaucracy went on forever.
They formed a self-perpetuating class of *literati* referred to by
Europeans as "mandarins."

The word *mandarin* itself was a European mispronunciation of
the Chinese words meaning "Manchu great man." Since Europeans arrived at Chinese ports in force only after the Manchu
conquest of the Celestial Empire, they adopted this word to
describe any and all of the rich literate Chinese government administrators (most of whom were not Manchus but Chinese
employed by the Manchu emperors). By that careless extension
which symptomized Europeans' disregard for the Asiatic cultures
they sought to dominate and exploit, the word was also applied
to the Vietnamese governing bureaucracy.

As in China, much of the wealth of Vietnam was agricultural.
If the king or emperor was to extract this wealth in the form of
taxes, a vast bookkeeping system was necessary as well as repre-
sentation of the royal authority in every part of the land. Only
the mandarin class could fulfill these functions. But this class was,
in turn, derived from the richest strata of farmers and merchants.
The mandarin landowners were naturally reluctant to tax themselves too heavily. When the king or emperor was strong they
could be brought to heel; when he was weak they would inevitably
shift their tax burden to the shoulders of their poorer neighbors or
tenants. This meant diminished taxes for the central government
and increased popular resentment against the regime. Eventually
these twin factors would bring about the collapse of the ruling
dynasty. Then a period of chaos would set in until a new leader,
capitalizing on the popular rebellion, would seize power, establish
his own dynasty—and start the cycle over again.

The great objectives of the mandarins, like bureaucrats everywhere, were to resist change and retain their power. To achieve these they would cooperate with any central authority that did not threaten their position. Thus, when from time to time the Chinese ruled the country, and when the French came, they found a ready-made and willing-to-serve governmental administration in existence. The mandarins preferred to rule their country on behalf of a foreign exploiting power rather than lose their wealth and privileges—all of which was very much on the traditional Chinese model.

But too strict a comparison between Vietnam and China would be false. Vietnam was not China, even during the periods of real or theoretical Chinese overlordship. For one thing, the pattern and structure of China's imperial government were very much older and very much more settled than Vietnam's. As we have seen, Vietnamese history from before the birth of Christ until the beginning of the nineteenth century was one of almost incessant expansion and warfare—which meant that *all* governmental authority was relatively weaker. The Vietnamese peasant living in his village commune enjoyed much more relative independence from central government interference and dictation than did his Chinese counterpart. On the other hand, he enjoyed fewer governmental benefits. It was not until the administration of the Emperor Gia Long at the beginning of the nineteenth century that a central Vietnamese government undertook on a large scale such national public works as flood control, a unified legal code, the establishment of a reliable postal system, etc.—all benefits age-old in China.

Another and extremely important difference between Vietnam and China was the relative social structure of the two nations. While, as in China, the great majority of Vietnamese were peasants, either farming their own small plots of land or share-cropping on the estates of the wealthy, a far larger proportion of the population than in China was engaged in trade and other commercial enterprises. While China was vast enough to be almost self-sufficient, much of the Vietnamese economy depended on trade—overland (in times of peace) with the peoples of Laos, Cambodia, Siam, Burma and even distant India, by sea to Malaya and the islands of the Indonesian archipelago. This meant that by the nineteenth century a much greater proportion of Vietnamese than Chinese were urban (concentrated in the port cities) and had developed into a nascent middle class of merchants and traders. A much larger proportion of the Vietnamese ruling bureaucracy was drawn from this class than were their Chinese counterparts, and since their interests were commercial rather than agricultural, Vietnamese merchant mandarins were eager to cooperate with European traders. Thus while China remained officially "closed" to both the trade and the influence of Europeans (who were confined to a single small port) for more than two centuries, Vietnamese ports were open to them; their trade and their presence were encouraged.

Yet another unique legacy of Vietnamese history was the presence within the country of nearly two and one-half million non-Vietnamese—more than ten percent of the population. These included, besides about 400,000 Chinese, the survivors of those peoples conquered over the centuries as the nation was unified. The Thai (700,000), the Muong (200,000), the Man (90,000) and the Meo (80,000) peoples lived in the northern mountains around the Red River delta. In the foothills they grew rice on terraced land; on high ground they raised livestock and grew opium. The authority of the central government grew weaker the farther it penetrated into the mountains, and the social organization of these highlanders was semifeudal, with strongmen and strong clans ruling over a serflike peasantry. Around the Mekong River delta in the south were to be found 300,000 Cambodians (conquered Khmers), and in the central mountains, 720,000 Moi tribesmen. The word "Moi" means "savages" in Vietnamese— and these were the descendants of the original Indonesian settlers who had been driven from the plains by successive waves of Vietnamese invaders. The Moi cultivated some rice on terraced land, but mostly they subsisted by gathering fruit and by fishing and hunting. They built their houses on stilts (against both the heavy rains and the snakes) and knew no governmental organization that went beyond their primitive villages.

If Vietnam was a mixture of peoples, it was also a mixture of cultures: Indian, Chinese and Indonesian. Hinduism, Buddhism, Taoism and Confucianism were the dominant religions of the country—but among the peasant millions all had been reduced, over the centuries, to one form or another of ancestor worship, the original, primitive and almost universal true Vietnamese religion. While the large cities and towns might boast temples dedicated to one or another of the prophets of these great oriental faiths, most Vietnamese worshipped before a household shrine devoted to the spirits of their forebears, and their rituals were simple, intimate and private. They did not demand too much of the gods (with whom their ancestors were supposed to intervene) —a better harvest, cure for sickness, the birth of a son, safety on a long journey; and they themselves hoped to rejoin their ancestors when they died, to assure which they strove to die and be buried at home.

If the average Vietnamese did not demand too much of his gods, it was because he did not expect too much of life. His staple food was rice, served with a pungent sauce made out of dried fish. This might be supplemented from time to time by fresh fish or game and an abundance of wild-growing fruit. His house was a structure of wood and bamboo built on stilts or on earth depending on his locality. He was prey to every variety of tropical disease, from malaria to the plague; his life expectancy was no more than thirty years. To achieve even this precarious existence he had to labor incessantly in his rice paddies. His natural enemies, aside from disease, were floods (the Red River's unpredictable rampages from time to time not only destroyed hundreds of thousands of acres of rice paddies but also drowned hundreds of thousands of people) and the jungle, which he had constantly to keep at bay.

His other enemies, so powerful and age-old as to almost constitute natural forces in themselves, were the government and the landlord—usually, on the village level, represented by one and the same person. To the government he owed taxes and, when military press gangs could catch him, service in the imperial army; to the landlord he owed rent. Since the average Vietnamese peasant had no money (he might live his entire life without setting eyes on that mysterious article), both his taxes and his rent were most often a share of the rice he cultivated, the animals he raised or the labor of which he was capable. Since he was illiterate he generally had to accept the landlord-mandarin's word as to how much he

owed, and he was rarely out of debt. When the central government was weak, his village council of elders might be able to
resist or escape some of the village's tax and rent obligations, but
in such times the village would be prey to roving bands of brigands
or disorganized soldiers. Rebellion against this order of things
(and rebellions were common) might lead to temporary relief,
but in the long run it seemed only to establish a new master family
in the distant capital and leave unchanged the rule of the local
landlord-mandarins.

The average Vietnamese city-dweller was not better off than
his peasant cousin. He lived in appalling slums where disease was
even more rampant than in the countryside; his wages were so low
that every member of the family had to work simply to survive—
and quite often he was forced to "sell" his children into semi-
slavery to prevent their starving. His grievances were the more
irritating because he was a daily witness to the life of the wealthy,
to their palaces, their fine clothes, their feasts and their sumptu-
ous rituals.

Such was Vietnam on the eve of French penetration and colo-
nialization of the country: only recently emerged from a two-
thousand-year conquest of the land, its ruling classes perhaps
more cosmopolitan than those of China, the vast mass of its
people suffering exploited lives as they had from time immemo-
rial. It was, in fact, an explosion of popular discontent that
furnished support to the Tay Son rebellion at the end of the
eighteenth century—the rebellion from which Nguyen Anh, fifteen-year-old heir of the "kings" of Hué, fled; the rebellion he was
to put down with French aid . . .

CLOSE-UP

Do Luc's Diary

ON MAY 4, 1961, a North Vietnamese soldier named Do Luc started to record his experiences and impressions on the pages of a homemade diary. He made entries when and where he could: sometimes on the march, sometimes encamped in the jungles or in the foothills of South Vietnam—any time he could snatch a few moments for himself. Beginning on August 15, 1961, Do Luc wrote:

"Memory!

"One afternoon which is turning into evening. I am sitting on the peak of a high mountain. This is a famous scenic place. This is the highest peak of the whole chain of mountains, and it is all covered with mist. All this scenery arouses nostalgia in my heart! I try to recall my life since I was a young boy.

"I answered the call of the Party [Communist Party] when I was very young, and what did I do for the people of my village? I devoted myself to the people. I took part in propaganda and aroused the people to carry out the policy of the Party and the Government and helped organize village defense and fighting

Do Luc's home was not far from the shores of Halong Bay.

Do Luc received his training in the People's Militia of North Vietnam.

forces. On March 25, 1954, I began my fighting career and I contributed my part in fighting the French Expeditionary Force.
With the army of Interzone 5, I saw the end of the war on July
20, 1954, and then on April 26, 1955, I left my native place and all
the ties with my family and friends to go North as a victorious
fighter. Since that day, my spirit has matured together with that
of the regular army. We have built up a beautiful and prosperous
and strong North; the construction sites and factories spring up
quickly everywhere under a bright sky and under the superior
socialist regime. Close to me there was a unique source of consola-
tion in my life. My life was beautiful, my happiness immeasurable. Enough to eat; warm clothing in my daily life; earning a
living was fairly easy; often I enjoyed songs and dances which
dealt with the healthy life of all the people in the North and with
the maturity of the Army.

"Then, one morning, while my life was touched with a fresh,
joyous and peaceful atmosphere, in harmony with the reconstruc-
tion program in the North, while my life was a normal one and I
was happy with my only love . . .

"Suddenly, on December 15, 1960, . . .

"I answered the needs of the international solidarity of the
Vietnamese-Laotian proletariat. I had to leave my beloved
Fatherland and my sweet life and go to help our friends with a
spirit of unselfishness, of class solidarity, of love for my Fatherland, and the spirit of the international proletarian revolution, in
order to annihilate the reactionary clique of Pumi Buon Um
[Phoumi-Boun Oum, leader of a Laotian political faction] so that
mankind and the two countries, Viet-Nam and Laos, could
achieve prosperity and happiness.

"Thus, I succeeded in meeting the needs of a friendly country.

"Our friends' war has stopped and the guns are silent. On the
call of the Party, I returned to my beloved Fatherland! My life
returned to normal. I enjoyed again the peaceful atmosphere and
my happiness. I continued training daily for the defense of the
territory of the North and for the continuation of the liberation
of the South. But I was back with my only love. Hurrah! How
happy and how sweet. But my life could not continue that way!

"For the third time my life turned to war again. For the liberation of our compatriots in the South, a situation of boiling oil and burning fire is necessary! A situation in which husband is separated from wife, father from son, brother from brother is necessary. I joined the ranks of the liberation army in answer to the call of the front for liberation of the South.

"Now my life is full of hardship—not enough rice to eat nor enough salt to give a taste to my tongue, not enough clothing to keep myself warm! But in my heart I keep loyal to the Party and to the people. I am proud and happy.

"I am writing down this story for my sons and my grandsons of the future to know of my life and activities during the revolution when the best medicine available was the root of the wild banana tree and the best bandage was the leaf of rau lui, when there was no salt to give a taste to our meals, when there was no such food as meat or fish like we enjoy in a time of peace and happiness such as I have known and left behind. But that day will not take long to return to my life."

At the end of his diary Do Luc listed "10 disciplinary rules for military security":

"1. Do not disclose army secrets. Do not be curious about your own responsibilities and duties.

"2. Do not discuss the duties you must carry out.

"3. You must respect absolutely the regulations which protect documents during your activities. Do not carry with you those things [such as diaries!] that regulations prohibit you from carrying. If you are captured by the enemy, be determined not to give in.

"Slogans: —absolute loyalty to the revolution;
              —death is preferable to slavery.

"4. Keep secret our method of hiding weapons.

"5. Do not take the liberty of listening to enemy broadcasts or of reading their newspapers or documents. Do not spread false rumors.

"6. Do not have any relations with any organization with evil segments of the population which are harmful to the revolution.

"7. Do not take your family or relatives or friends to military campsites.

"8. Keep order and security among the population as well as among yourselves.

"9. Do not cease to carry out self-criticism or being vigilant, and continue your training.

"10. Implement seriously these ten rules, mentally as well as in deeds."

Do Luc was killed in the central Vietnamese highlands in the fall of 1961. His captured diary was translated and published, along with several others, by the United States State Department in December of that same year.

Chapter Two

THE PARIS OF THE ORIENT

France is a strange country. It is a breeding
ground of admirable ideas, but when it travels,
it does not export them . . .

—HO CHI MINH

IN ITS long history the palace at Versailles has known some
memorable occasions, but surely one of the strangest scenes its
baroque halls ever witnessed took place on November 27, 1787.
For on that day, under the friendly auspices of French bishop
Pigneau de Behaine, King Louis XVI, His Most Christian Maj-
esty, heir of the Bourbons, still ruler of one of the most powerful
nations in Europe, signed a treaty of friendship and aid with
Nguyen Anh, the dispossessed "king" of Hué, a tiny part of a land
so far from France as to be almost as legendary as the nonexistent
empire of Prester John. The contrast between the splendidly
robed courtiers of King Louis and the long-robed Vietnamese
mandarins must have been exotic indeed. The impoverished
Nguyen Anh (his lands still in the power of the Tay Son rebels)
was definitely in the position of a supplicant before the power of
France. He hoped to use that power to win back his kingdom. On
the other hand, Louis XVI and his advisors hoped that through
their aid to Nguyen Anh they might begin to win for France an
oriental empire to replace the North American and Indian hold-
ings they had lost to England. Yet almost everything about that
splendid scene at Versailles was misleading. Louis XVI was

32

already embroiled in domestic difficulties that within two years were to lead to the great French Revolution. The pomp and power of the Ancient Regime so glitteringly displayed that day at Versailles was only a brittle sham. And long after it had been swept away, years after Louis XVI's well-meaning but addled head had been severed from its body, the supplicant Nguyen Anh was to rule as a powerful emperor over a united Vietnam.

The French were not the first Europeans to reach Vietnam. It was the Portuguese who first found the route around the Cape of Good Hope and sailed their cockleshell galleons to the coasts of India, Burma, Indonesia and, in the middle of the sixteenth century, Vietnam. As Portuguese fortunes in Europe declined during the late sixteenth and early seventeenth centuries, their monopoly of the eastern trade was broken and then seized by the expanding power of Holland and England. By the middle of the seventeenth century both the Dutch and the English had established trading posts at Hanoi. The French, vying with England for control of the rich Orient trade, soon followed. French Catholic missionaries were active in Vietnam all during the seventeenth century; one of them, Alexandre de Rhodes, adapted the Vietnamese language to the Roman alphabet to produce the *quoc-ngu*, a means of writing Vietnamese in western alphabetical rather than pictograph style.

For these early European merchants, the risk of the months-long sea voyage and the discomforts and dangers of life among a totally alien people were amply rewarded by the profits they made. Established at Hanoi, not only could they trade for Vietnamese tea and rare woods and spices, but here they could also come by the rich products of China, a land still closed to European trade. And from the ports of Vietnam their frail sailing ships could ply the China Sea to the rich islands of the south.

To the European governments of France, England and Holland, their merchant adventurers in the Far East were more than private citizens; they were national representatives, integral parts of the national economic policy. During the sixteenth, seventeenth and eighteenth centuries that economic policy went under the name of mercantilism. According to the mercantilist view, national wealth was to be measured strictly by the amount of gold

and silver in the national treasury (how else could the king pay
his mercenary armies, support his expensive navies?)—and the
overriding aim of national economic policy was simply to increase
that hoard of precious metals. To this end colonies, wherever
situated, existed only to be milked by the mother country. Trade
with the rich Orient provided so important a part of the revenues
of those nations lucky or powerful enough to partake in it that
they would defend it at any cost, even full-scale war. Yet lucrative
as eastern trade was, how much more lucrative would be the
exploitation of oriental wealth through the establishment of colonies! For two centuries the European powers fought each other
for control of oriental trade; for more than one hundred years
England and France fought to see which of them would inherit
the decayed empire of the Moguls in India. By the end of the
eighteenth century France had lost Canada, Louisiana and all but
a foothold in India to British power. It was understandable then
that the government of Louis XVI was eager to establish its influence in Vietnam.

That influence made itself felt very quickly. Nguyen Anh, now
aided by French money, French ships and, above all, French military officers from the French toehold in India, was able to defeat
the Tay Son rebels, advance northward and enter Hanoi in triumph in 1802. There, adopting the name of Gia Long, he established a new dynasty to rule over all of Vietnam. As a reward he
gave to France the port of Tourane and the southern coastal island
of Poulo Condor. He also, of course, favored French trade and
commerce, protected French missionaries and encouraged the
adoption of French learning and modes of behavior among his
courtiers, the inevitably inherited mandarin bureaucracy. Gia
Long proved an able ruler, undertaking numerous public works, a
land survey and the promulgation of a new legal code—all with
French advice. Nor did the emperor ever forget his obligation to
his French friends. When the venerable missionary bishop
Pigneau de Behaine died in 1799, Gia Long, though still engaged
in his struggle to gain the imperial throne, personally supervised
the construction of his friend's tomb in Saigon and wrote a suitable epitaph for it himself.

Yet it was Gia Long's admiration for things French and friendship for his benefactors that were to bring about conflict between his subjects and France. It will be recalled that the Vietnamese Empire was administered by an all but hereditary class of land-lord-mandarins. These would serve any master, even a foreign one, provided always that their position in relation to the rest of the population was preserved inviolate. At first, the slow expansion of French trading enterprises in the empire, the influence of French Catholic missionaries, and the growing French military "presence" based on Tourane and Poulo Condor did not seem to seriously threaten the mandarins' role. Indeed, those of the mandarin class whose wealth derived from commerce rather than land profited. As for Catholicism—the Vietnamese accepted (or neglected) this as just another of the religions competing within the empire. But although Vietnamese converts to the western faith were few, it was observed that these left the schools of the missionary fathers literate, far better educated than their peasant compatriots, and with attitudes that questioned the age-old domination of the mandarin-landlord hierarchy. Furthermore, as French commercial interests spread in Vietnam, French traders and businessmen were increasingly exploiting the national wealth directly—through the establishment of tea and coffee plantations, direct trade with peasants for rare wood and spices, etc.—without dealing through the mandarin merchants of Hanoi, Hué and Saigon, or the landlord-mandarins of the interior. All of which seriously threatened the domination of Vietnamese society by its native governing class. Accordingly, the mandarins, generally secretly but often openly, struck back.

The mandarins' weapon against the French was Vietnamese nationalism. They were able to persuade large numbers of the populace that French influence was but the precursor of French conquest—to equate the French with the traditional Vietnamese enemy, China (which still claimed, though it could not exercise, authority over the Hanoi regime). Under the reign of Gia Long, mandarin-inspired resentment against the French was kept to very modest proportions. But Gia Long's successors (the old emperor died in 1820), increasingly fearful of French penetration as a threat to their own power, secretly abetted a growing resistance to it. This took the form, under the Emperor Minh-Mang (1820–

1841), of the murder of French Catholic missionaries. When the Emperor Tu Doc ascended the throne in 1848 the persecution was intensified. Between 1833 and 1873 fifteen missionary priests and no less than eight European bishops were put to death. But the real weight of the persecutions fell on native Vietnamese Christians, who perished by the thousands over the years.

French reaction to these events depended very much on domestic conditions in metropolitan France. The France that had been bled white by the Napoleonic wars and had gone through the revolutionary upheavals of 1830, 1836 and 1848 displayed neither the power nor the interest to intervene forcefully in distant Asia. But with the coming to power of Napoleon III (proclaimed emperor of the French in 1852) matters changed. France was then undergoing widespread industrialization. Large amounts of new capital were required—and larger profits would follow. The French commercial interest in distant Vietnam now assumed a new significance in the eyes of French businessmen and administrators. Furthermore, as the megalomaniac inheritor of a great imperial name, Napoleon III could not tolerate the abuse of any of his subjects, especially by "inferior" orientals. The new emperor of the French soon concluded that personal glory, commercial advantage and domestic political support required the re-creation of a French overseas empire. Algeria, West Africa, the Pacific islands, even Mexico (a conquest that failed) were to provide the new imperial domains. And in the Far East there was Vietnam, where an "ungrateful" population had murdered French subjects, thereby providing a perfect excuse for French intervention.

This intervention assumed the concrete shape of a Franco-Spanish Expeditionary Force (one of the murdered bishops, it seems, had been a Spaniard) of warships and troop transports commanded by French Admiral Charles Rigault de Genouilly. Admiral Rigault's forces landed and occupied Saigon in 1859—only to find themselves besieged in that city by an aroused peasantry cooperating with imperial forces from Hanoi. It was not until the arrival of heavy reinforcements from France in 1861 that Rigault's forces were able to break the siege and advance into the country-side. By a treaty signed with Emperor Tu Doc on June 5, 1862, the three coastal provinces of southern Vietnam, including the great port city of Saigon, were ceded to France. The French promptly named their new colony Cochin China and established a military administration headed by a series of admirals.

In 1863 neighboring Cambodia, facing a Siamese invasion from the west, made the fatal mistake of seeking French protection. The protection was supplied speedily, the Siamese were discouraged, and on August 11, 1863, a French "protectorate" was proclaimed over Cambodia. The Cambodian king was permitted to retain his throne, but a French governor general supported by French troops really ruled the country. Three years later the French forces in "Cochin China" overran the western provinces of that area, and French rule extended over all of the southern portion of Vietnam as well as Cambodia—over all the ancient territories of the Khmers.

A sharp taste of what the future might hold was received by Emperor Tu Doc in 1873. Perhaps influenced by news from Europe of France's defeat at the hands of Prussia in 1870 and the abdication and flight of Napoleon III, Tu Doc and his mandarins made bold to harass certain French commercial enterprises within the emperor's domains (Tu Doc still ruled over northern and central Vietnam). But the newly established Third French Republic, whatever its democratic pretensions at home, showed itself as imperial-minded as Napoleon III's Second Empire had been. Tu Doc's interference with French merchants was speedily punished. An expedition headed by Francis Garnier seized Hanoi in November 1873 and then set about subduing the rest of the area around the Red River delta. But in December 1873 Garnier was killed in battle. It is interesting to note that he was killed not by Vietnamese forces, but by Chinese irregulars called in by the desperate Tu Doc. These Chinese forces were called Black Flag Brigands by the French—to indicate that they were simply bandits acting from motives of personal greed. But the Vietnamese regarded them as allies and heroes. Actually they were "volunteer" guerrillas secretly supported by the Chinese Empire to prevent a French take-over of northern Vietnam, an area vital to Chinese border security and one which, it must be remembered, was still theoretically a Chinese vassal state.

Garnier's death and the intervention of the Black Flag Brigands seemed to provoke second thoughts in Saigon and Paris. The French conquests of Hanoi and the Red River delta area were renounced and French forces withdrawn. In return for this, Tu Doc promised to "conform his policy" more closely to that of France, to cease his harassment of French merchants and to grant them trading rights on the river routes into southern China. But the guerrilla activities of the Black Flag Brigands continued; their ranks were constantly reinforced not only by Chinese but also by Vietnamese rebels. It was apparent that the French would sooner or later undertake another expedition to subdue them. In a desperate attempt to forestall such a move, Tu Doc publicly and officially reaffirmed his vassalage to the Chinese Empire in 1880. Unfortunately, this (to the Vietnamese) highly distasteful step was of no use. The Chinese Empire was itself under attack by various European powers; its strength was insufficient to maintain even its own territorial and political integrity.

The inevitable French expedition appeared once more off the delta of the Red River in 1882. Hanoi was captured in April of that year and large areas of northern Vietnam conquered. The following year the French launched an attack on central Vietnam and easily captured Hué. On August 25, 1883, Tu Doc signed a treaty with the French by which the latter finally established a protectorate over all of Vietnam. As in Cambodia, the emperor was permitted to retain his throne, but real power was henceforth to be exercised by French representatives. To deal with the Black Flag Brigands, the French went directly to the source of the disturbance. Military action (and the threat of more) convinced the tottering Chinese Empire (now reeling beneath the weight of European imperialistic pressures, harassments and attacks) to sign a convention with France at Tientsin on May 11, 1884, whereby they agreed to withdraw all Chinese forces, regular or irregular, and to recognize the French protectorate over Vietnam.

The Chinese withdrew from northern Vietnam (after first inflicting a crushing defeat on overeager French forces attempting to hurry them along at Lang Son), but peace did not follow. Vietnamese guerrillas replaced the Black Flag Brigands, and the mandarins who controlled the government of Tu Doc's successors (the old emperor had died in 1883) never ceased to conspire against the French. Their ill-advised attack on French forces in Hué in July 1885 led the exasperated French to restrict the Vietnamese Empire to central Vietnam, the area called Annam with its capital at Hué, and to install their own puppet emperor, Dong Khanh, on the throne of this Annamese Empire. All subsequent emperors in Vietnam were to be completely subservient to the interests of France.

The great French colony of Indochina, which took definitive shape during the closing years of the nineteenth century, was organized into five separate districts. Northern Vietnam was now called Tonkin and was ruled directly as a French colony; central Vietnam was the "independent" Empire of Annam ruled by an emperor but completely controlled by French officials; southern Vietnam was named Cochin China and was ruled, like the north, directly by French administrators. The Kingdom of Cambodia and the Kingdom of Laos (annexed as a protectorate in 1893) were, like the Empire of Annam, independent in name only. Over all these regions presided a French governor general for all of Indochina who was the head of the colonial administration, controlled the armed forces, approved the separate budgets of the five regions, and was France's official representative in Indochina.

The administration of justice throughout Indochina was based, in principle, on French law; but cases that did not involve Europeans were generally heard before native courts administering justice according to the traditions of the local region. Europeans, of course, in Indochina as in other parts of the Far East during this heyday of European imperialism, did not come under native law. They could only be tried or heard before French courts administering French law. Only rarely could a Vietnamese hope to win a claim against a European before such tribunals.

The impact of France upon the people, culture, social structure and economy of Vietnam was profound and apparently lasting. French was proclaimed a second "official" language and taught compulsorily in the public schools that the French established. Most educated Vietnamese read and spoke it fluently. The Catholic religion was granted recognition along with Buddhism, Hinduism, Confucianism and other native sects, and protected from persecution. Eventually Vietnamese Catholics would number more than two million, and the impact of Christianity upon the native faiths would lead to such interesting latter-day religions as Cao-Dai, an attempt to fuse Buddhist and Christian doctrines.

The governments of the different regions of Vietnam differed in detail, but basic to all of them was the suppression of the power of the mandarin ruling class. Local and regional administration and services were overwhelmingly staffed by Vietnamese, and among them, of course, were included those mandarins who would accept French direction. But the powers of taxation, conscription and expenditure of public funds were now thoroughly centralized in French hands. Mandarin landlords now paid their taxes to Saigon, and though corruption was rife (and tacitly tolerated by the French), the mandarin no longer combined in his own person the powers of both the wealthy landowner or merchant and the government official. Furthermore, the individual economic power of members of the old ruling class grew feebler and feebler as French merchants, landowners, industrialists and businessmen gradually penetrated and then dominated the Vietnamese economy.

The French economic exploitation of Indochina was thorough and extremely successful. The rice-growing economy of the southern Mekong River delta area was expanded until by 1939 Indochina was able to export nearly 1,700,000 tons of this staple—making the French colony the third largest rice exporter in the world. The mines of northern Indochina were made to produce healthy quantities of coal, iron, manganese and zinc. And although the establishment of heavy industry was not encouraged (Indochina was meant to buy most of its manufactured goods from France), factories did spring up around Hanoi, close to their sources of raw materials, the mines. Of tremendous consequence to the French and world economies were the great rubber plantations of Cochin China. Until the development of rubber substitutes during World War II, Indochina was one of the world's leading exporters of this vital material. Both the French and to a very large extent the Japanese industrial economies depended on this source—with consequences that were to prove unhappy for both nations. Tea, coffee, spices, rare woods, hides, corn—all these were among the profitable products of a naturally fertile and relatively unexploited land. And the French merchants and businessmen who flocked into Indochina after its subjugation made certain that these riches flowed to them. There was enough—even enough to bribe the native mandarins and buy out native merchants and landowners. Many a French fortune (as witness the Michelin rubber products industry, one of the world's largest) was wrested from the colonial economy. Indochinese exports in 1939, for example, were valued at nearly three and a half billion francs—most of which went to the French owners of the Indochinese economy. On the other hand, Indochinese imports (of manufactured goods and petroleum products) were valued at nearly two and a half billion francs—most of which went to French domestic industries. Altogether a praiseworthy system, from the French viewpoint.

This French economic exploitation was not without certain benefits also for native Vietnamese. To get at the country's riches more efficiently, the French built railroads and highways and developed the ports, especially Haiphong near Hanoi and the harbor of Saigon. A public-school system on the French model was established and more than a few hospitals were built. French doctors waged a selfless war against malaria and other common tropical diseases. A healthy French-speaking modestly educated native Vietnamese population could only be an asset to the colonial administration. Yet it must not be supposed that all the French civil servants who toiled in Indochina were cynically motivated. Very many considered that by bringing to the Orient France's great culture and civilization they were conferring immeasurable benefits—and to a certain extent they were right. Furthermore, most Frenchmen did not suffer from blatant racism, that disease so prevalent among colonizing Englishmen, Germans and Americans. While Vietnamese might not be admitted to the most exclusive Saigon clubs (most Frenchmen were excluded too), there was a noticeable absence throughout Indochina of such manifestations of racist psychology as the "No dogs or Chinese admitted" signs to be seen everywhere in Hong Kong, Shanghai, Singapore and other centers of white European domination. The streets of Hanoi and Saigon were broadened and

paved and public transportation systems provided. With its out-
door cafes, its advertising signs in French, its cinemas and theaters
and public squares, Saigon could claim to be the "Paris of the
Orient."

And yet the flames of Vietnamese resistance to French domination were never fully stamped out. Groups such as the Phuc Quoc,
the Van Than and the Dong Du maintained a constant spirit of
rebellion and did not shrink from violence when it appeared necessary or useful. For France was not seen as the bringer of a new
and higher civilization. That was a role she might affect for the
natives of Senegal or African Gabon, but the Vietnamese were
proud of their own very sophisticated, highly advanced and an-
ciently rooted culture. Except to a handful of ambitious intellectuals, French culture and civilization were felt to be but a small
and unwanted contribution in the face of French oppression.

The remarkable economic development carried out by the
French was accomplished with the conscript labor of hundreds
of thousands of Vietnamese. French police would round up the
able-bodied inhabitants of entire districts to be sent to forced
labor on the new roads or railroads or port facilities. From the
populous north huge gangs of "coolies" were sent to work the
new rubber plantations of the south. Only the fact that these impressed workers were paid a few cents a day wages made their life
any different from that of slaves. And while the lot of the conscripted workers was terrible (the hard labor, jungles where the
temperature rarely fell below 100°, the overseer's lash, the bowl of
rice and little else, the lack of shelter), the lives of their uncon-
scripted fellow countrymen were not much better. Very many
peasants, indeed entire village communities, lost their land to the
French plantation masters. They could then either work as agricultural day laborers or seek a new life in the cities. But the appalling slums that spread around Hanoi, Haiphong, Hué and Saigon
were mute testimony to the harshness and despair of the lives of
the urban poor.

And, of course, as part of the French Empire, Indochina was
expected to take part in France's wars. Many Vietnamese, from
the earliest days of French rule, were conscripted to fight against
their Laotian, Cambodian and Siamese neighbors, that these

nations too might fall under French domination. During the First World War hundreds of thousands of Vietnamese were conscripted into huge labor armies, shipped to metropolitan France, and set to work digging trenches, carrying supplies, growing food for the troops, and occasionally serving as cannon fodder in the flaming front lines—all in the service of a cause utterly foreign to Vietnamese experience, needs or hopes.

The France that was seen by most Vietnamese was the France of corrupt petty officials, of oppressive police, of greedy tax collectors, of recruiting sergeants, of the brutal ranks of the French Foreign Legion. It was the France that crushed all political opposition ruthlessly, the France that maintained, on the island of Poulo Condor, one of the world's most notorious penal colonies —a veritable oriental Devil's Island to which many were condemned but from which very few returned alive. For every Vietnamese businessman who profited through French rule, for every Vietnamese clerk glad to find a job with the French administration, for every Vietnamese scholar impressed by French culture, there were thousands of Vietnamese who hated their new overlords and awaited only the day of liberation.

A Case of Conscience

"ANY PERSON who knowingly counsels, aids or abets another to refuse or evade registration or service in the Armed Forces . . . shall be liable to imprisonment for not more than five years or a fine of ten thousand dollars or both."—*National Selective Service Act, Section 12.*

The time: October 20, 1967 (midafternoon, a chilly wind rushing clouds across a raw sky). The place: the steps of the Justice Department building in Washington, D. C. (police lines carefully drawn to hold back a small group of onlookers, batteries of television cameras carefully arranged to expand that audience a millionfold). The participants: several hundred college students from every part of the United States, as well as college professors, faculty advisors and a handful of notables (writer Norman Mailer, poet Robert Lowell, critic Dwight MacDonald, medical specialist Dr. Benjamin Spock and others). Purpose of the gathering: to protest in the most public and vigorous manner possible America's continuing war in Vietnam.

Conscience meets force outside the Pentagon.

The proceedings are not complicated. Yale University Chaplain William Sloan Coffin makes a brief speech condemning the morality of American intervention in Vietnam. Then, one by one, students and faculty members and some of the celebrities present step forward to drop their draft cards into a large bag. Chaplain Coffin, reading from a prepared text, declares: "We hereby publicly counsel these young men to continue in their refusal to serve in the armed forces as long as the war in Vietnam continues, and we pledge ourselves to aid and abet them in all the ways we can. This means that if they are now arrested for failing to comply with a law that violates their consciences, we too must be arrested, for in the sight of the law we are now as guilty as they."

With 994 draft cards in the bag (and many affidavits sworn to by students declaring that they have previously burned their draft cards) Chaplain Coffin, Dr. Spock and a representative group of demonstrators enter the Justice Department building. They are determined to present themselves, along with their self-incriminating evidence, to the attorney general of the United States and demand that he prosecute them to the full extent of the law.

After a while Chaplain Coffin, Dr. Spock and other members of the delegation emerge from the Justice Department. Their faces reflect anger, disappointment and bewilderment. The attorney general is not "in." Instead they have been greeted by an assistant attorney general who has refused point-blank to accept their bag of draft cards and affidavits.

"Consider this," Chaplain Coffin reports to the crowd of demonstrators and onlookers waiting on the Justice Department steps. "Here is an officer of the law facing clear evidence of an alleged crime, and refusing to accept that evidence. He was derelict in his duty!"

But the dereliction was merely temporary. Within a few months Chaplain Coffin, Dr. Spock and many of their co-demonstrators were to be arrested, tried and convicted of willfully violating the Selective Service Act.

> con-science (kon'shuns), n. ideas and feeling
> within a person that warn him of what is wrong.
> —*Thorndike-Barnhart Dictionary*

Chapter Three

THE DELEGATE FROM INDOCHINA

It's impossible to forget the presence at the Congress of an Indochinese delegate then living in France . . . he called on the Socialists to lend support to the downtrodden, hampered, butchered, poisoned native population. Who was this delegate from the Far East? None other than Ho Chi Minh.

—MARCEL CACHIN

BETWEEN ANNAM (central Vietnam) and Tonkin (the north) lies the region and province of Nghe-Trinh—an area famous for its dense population, its deep poverty, and the rebelliousness of its inhabitants. It is known as "the land of the wooden fish." In earlier days a man setting out from Nghe-Trinh on a journey would put a small wooden fish into his pocket. When he stopped to eat at a wayside inn, being too poor to order anything more, he would ask for a plain bowl of rice and a bowl of *nuoc-mam*, the national condiment. But in order not to appear too poor to the other guests, the traveler from Nghe-Trinh would slyly slip his little wooden fish into the *nuoc-mam*, thereby giving the impression of a man feasting substantially. And since the wooden fish soaked up some of the spicy pickle juice, it would be pleasant to lick later on while hiking down the road.

So dense is the population of Nghe-Trinh, and so deep their poverty (many families must support themselves from the proceeds of a rice paddy no larger than a quarter of an acre), that for centuries ambitious children have studied hard for a career in

47

government service—their only potential route of escape. They might become scribes or schoolteachers or even win appointment to the emperor's court. But applicants from Nghe-Trinh were looked upon with suspicion by the mandarins of Hanoi and Hué: too often they proved themselves troublemakers and revolutionaries. Indeed, most of the rebellions and uprisings against Chinese overlordship, domestic oppression and, later, French domination originated in Nghe-Trinh. It was from Nghe-Trinh in 1885 that the rebel Phan Dinh Phung led the mandarin-inspired Scholars' Revolt against French colonialism; from this province too came the nationalist pamphleteer Phan Boi Chau, the reformer Phan Chu Trinh and both Tran Phu and Le Hong Phong, the first two general secretaries of the Indochinese Communist Party.

It was in this turbulent province, in the village of Kim Lien, on May 19, 1890, that a son was born into the family of Nguyen Sinh Huy, a mandarin of great learning who had been dismissed from his government post because of his anti-French opinions. The name given Nguyen Sinh Huy's son at birth was Nguyen Tat Thanh; later the son would adopt the alias Nguyen Ai Quoc and from time to time other, more obscure names. To avoid confusion we shall refer to him throughout by that revolutionary *nom de guerre* through which he became world-famous: Ho Chi Minh.

Ho's childhood made him acquainted both with poverty (after his dismissal from government, old Nguyen Sinh Huy became a wandering scribe; Ho's mother died when Ho was ten years old) and with the revolutionary traditions of his native province. Both Ho's sister and his brother were active in guerrilla movements against the French; the great pamphleteer Phan Boi Chau was a close friend of the family. Ho never forgot Phan Boi Chau's advice: those who wish to liberate the country must form a strong party.

At the age of fifteen Ho entered Quoc Hoc secondary school, one of the new French-built schools (its headmaster was an ex-Foreign Legionnaire), where he received his first real taste of French learning. It was probably at Quoc Hoc that young Ho discovered that France had a revolutionary tradition of its own; certainly such "subversive'" French authors as Voltaire, Michelet, Montesquieu and Rousseau would have been part of the curricu-

Ho Chi Minh in 1954.

lum. Given this discovery, combined with Ho's family and provincial background, it is not surprising that the young student from Nghe-Trinh would become involved in the local insurrectional movements that troubled the area in 1908.

In 1909 Ho traveled south to the port city of Phan Tiet. There he taught both *quoc ngu* (the alphabetized Vietnamese language) and French for a while. But in 1911 he again headed south —this time to Saigon, where he enrolled himself in a vocational school to learn marine navigation. It seems that he intended to work his way as a seaman to China, where the revolution of 1911 had just broken out. But two months after arriving at Saigon, Ho found a berth as a messboy on the French liner *Latouche-Treville*, a boat plying the Haiphong-Marseilles route. Ho was now twenty-one years old, and, like the men of Ireland, Italy and Yunnan

Province in China, poverty had driven him to seek a new life
abroad.

Ho's seagoing career took him over much of the world. He
visited all the big African and Mediterranean ports as well as
Marseilles, Boston and New York. He was able to see that French
imperialism had the same results in such places as Dakar and Port
Said as it had in Vietnam. His experiences at this time were later
to form the basis of his first book, *The Process of French Coloni-
zation*, a ringing indictment of France's overseas record. But at
Marseilles Ho also observed that the average person of metropolitan France was far different, far more sympathetic than the
colonial policemen, soldiers and administrators who were respon-
sible for furthering French interests in Vietnam.

In 1913 Ho decided to quit the sea. He made his way to
London, where, besides perfecting his English, he eked out a
living by washing dishes and shoveling snow. There is a legend
that he also worked as an assistant cook under the great French
chef Escoffier at London's exclusive Carlton Hotel. Be that as it
may, Ho found time in London also to join a secret organization
of oriental expatriates, the Lao Dong Hoi Nagai (Overseas Workers Organization), study the Irish revolutionary movement and
read the works of the English Fabian Socialists. These Fabian
writers, such as Sydney and Beatrice Webb and George Bernard
Shaw, proposed that a socialist intellectual elite use the democratic process to infiltrate government and, once in power, bring
about evolutionary social change. This advice was exactly contrary
to that which Ho had received from Phan Boi Chau: form a
strong party. Yet Ho's years in London brought him, for the first
time, into contact with revolutionary European socialist thought;
without that experience he might have remained simply another
Vietnamese nationalist, his horizons limited to the expulsion of
the French.

In 1917, perhaps realizing that nothing he did in England could
influence events in Vietnam, Ho moved to Paris. Despite the
indescribable agony of the First World War, then raging, he con-
ceived it possible that, in alliance with the many hundreds of
thousands of Vietnamese who had been drafted and shipped to
France for both combat and forced labor, he might be able to

influence Vietnamese affairs in the capital of his country's oppressor.

During the next five years Ho was to know extreme poverty. But he was also to realize that the French working class and French Socialists could be his most effective allies in his struggle against French imperialism. He soon established contact with leftist groups in Paris and for the first time began seriously to study the Communist classics, the works of Marx, Engels, Kautsky and Lenin. For a while he earned his living as a photographer. "If you would like a lifelike memento of your family, have your photos retouched at Nguyen Ai Quoc's. A lovely portrait in a lovely frame for 45 francs," read his advertisement in *La Vie Ouvriere*, a French leftist newspaper. It was during these years that Ho adopted the name Nguyen Ai Quoc, which means simply Nguyen the Patriot in Vietnamese.

Soon Ho began contributing articles to the Communist newspaper *L'Humanité* ("Reminiscences of an Exile"); he also wrote a morally earnest play, *The Bamboo Dragon*. He became the first Annamese member of the French Young Socialist movement. His compatriot Ho Van Tao described him at this time:

"He was still just an obscure photographer who had difficulty making a living. . . . A small, frail young man with a gaunt face and an expression of great gentleness, aglow with the flame which so often burns in the eyes of people who are exalted by an idea. . . . He was highly emotional. . . . For reasons which are not clear, some of his friends in those days used to call him 'little Monsieur Ferdinand.' "

It was during this time that Ho was first enlisted as a member of the Second International, that organization of Socialist parties of every country from which Lenin's Communists had withdrawn because of its "bourgeoise orientation." It was also at this time that the French secret police, the *Sureté*, began to take an interest in the fiery Vietnamese nationalist. Through his newspaper articles and pamphlets and through personal contact, he had become something of an influence among the many thousands of Vietnamese living in France. In fact he had not hesitated to present himself at the peace conference in Versailles with a set of eight demands for his country's emancipation. This eight-point

program asked basically that Vietnamese be accorded the same
rights as Frenchmen—a modest proposal based on President
Woodrow Wilson's Fourteen Points, which were supposed to
form the basis for the Versailles peace conference. But when Ho
attempted to see Wilson personally, he was unceremoniously
booted out. His program was, of course, completely disregarded
by the victorious Allies—but not by Vietnamese living in France,
who recognized it and its author as a new force in their lives.

It is not difficult to trace Ho's route from nationalist to Fabian
socialist to socialist. His overruling principle had always been:
What means of political expression will most quickly and effectively bring about the emancipation of Vietnam? In 1921 he
attended a Congress of Socialist Parties held at Tours, France,
which discussed, among other matters, whether or not to join the
Third (Communist) International. Ho was more interested,
however, in what these Socialists were prepared to do about liberating his native country. He made a memorable speech in which
he outlined French oppression in Indochina and called upon his
fellow Socialists: "On behalf of the whole of mankind, on behalf
of all the Socialist Party's members, both left and right wings, we
call upon you! Comrades, save us!"

Ho was not long to remain a Second-International Socialist.
He read Lenin's *Thesis on the National and Colonial Questions*
and joined the ninth cell of the newly formed French Communist
Party. Forty years later, recalling his path to communism in an
article published on the occasion of his seventieth birthday, Ho
wrote:

"At first, patriotism, not yet Communism, led me to have confidence in Lenin, in the Third International. Step by step, along
the struggle, by studying Marxism-Leninism parallel with participation in practical activities, I gradually came upon the fact that
only Socialism and Communism can liberate the oppressed nations and the working people of the world from slavery.

". . . Leninism is . . . a compass for us Vietnamese revolutionaries and people: it is also the radiant sun illuminating our path
to final victory, to Socialism and Communism."

Lenin's motive in establishing the Third International in Moscow had been simply this: according to Marxist analysis, the

Russian revolution was to have sparked off Communist revolutions throughout Europe. Indeed, without such revolutions in the highly industrial western nations, it had been doubtful whether the Communist regime could survive in war-torn, agricultural and backward Russia. But despite uprisings in Germany, Austria and Hungary, the awaited Communist revolutions in the West failed to take place. In fact, the firmly entrenched capitalist regimes of western Europe posed a dire threat to the young Russian Communist government. By setting up a new international organization of Communist parties, especially emphasizing Communist parties in the colonies of those western capitalist nations, Lenin and his associates hoped to be able to stir up enough trouble to keep the hostile western nations too busy to launch an attack on Russia itself. But this reasoning was not entirely self-serving, for Lenin himself had long since worked out the Marxist position on colonial exploitation. In his remarkable work, *Imperialism, the Last Stage of Capitalism*, Lenin had pointed out that such nations as France, England and the United States had so developed that they might now be considered capitalist entities despite the fact that each contained a working class. As nations they exploited a new working class that was none other than the populations of their various colonies. When this exploitation came to an end, through colonial revolutions and wars between the greedy imperialist nations, then the domestic capitalist structure of these countries would also collapse. In other words, the road to international Communist revolution now led through the colonies. Ho Chi Minh, uniquely experienced as both an exploited Vietnamese revolutionary and a comrade of the French revolutionary left in France, could not but agree.

But Ho Chi Minh was never to meet Lenin. After devoting himself for a few more years to publishing various newspapers and pamphlets in the cause of Vietnamese independence and communism, Ho left Paris for Moscow, arriving in January 1924 a few days after Lenin's death. Like so many other facts about Ho Chi Minh's revolutionary past, the date of his arrival in Moscow has been the occasion of some dispute, but January 1924 seems most probable. In any event, on January 27, 1924, the Russian newspaper *Pravda* published an article by Ho on Lenin's death

("Lenin is dead. What are we going to do? That is the question the oppressed masses in the colonies are anxiously asking themselves . . .").

Ho lived in the Soviet Union throughout 1924, attending courses at Moscow's University of the Toilers of the East and meeting many of Lenin's old associates, including Joseph Stalin who, as former People's Commissar of Nationalities, had taken particular interest in colonial problems. As a delegate to the Fifth Congress of the Third (Communist) International held in Moscow from June 17 to July 8, 1924, Ho made an extremely favorable impression on his fellow-delegates. Addressing them, he struck a new note by emphasizing the role that peasants (as opposed to urban industrial workers) might be expected to play in revolutionary movements in the colonies.

"The revolt of the colonial peasants is imminent," Ho proclaimed. "They have already risen in several colonies, but each time their rebellions have been drowned in blood. If they now seem resigned, that is solely for lack of organization and leadership. It is the duty of the Communist International to work toward their union. . . ." These words would seem to foreshadow the new and unorthodox policies that Mao Tse-tung and Ho himself later followed to revolutionary success.

In January 1925 Ho was sent as secretary (and "Asia expert") with the Russian revolutionary Mikhail Borodin to Canton in China. Borodin's mission was to advise and assist Chiang Kai-shek, then allied with the Communists, in his effort to unify China, conquer the warlords and establish a democratic republic. But Ho Chi Minh seems to have spent more time on Indochinese politics than on the Chinese revolution. Canton was then a hotbed of exiled Vietnamese patriots, and Ho set himself the task of educating them in the socialist view of revolution; "Assassinating Governors General is not the way to achieve the overthrow of the colonial regime. To secure victory for the revolution a powerful party is needed. . . ."

Six months after arriving in Canton, Ho, along with several friends, established the *Vietnam Thanh Nien Cach Mang Dong Chi Hoi* (Association of Vietnamese Revolutionary Youth)— generally abbreviated to Thanh Nien—which was to become the nucleus of the Indochinese Communist Party. But Ho realized that for the moment Thanh Nien would have to adopt moderate views if it was to appeal to the tradition-bound peasants and workers of the south. In *The Road to Revolution* (1926) Ho stressed three themes:

"1. The revolution is a task for the broad working-class and peasant masses, not for a handful of men. Hence the need to organize the masses.

"2. The revolution must be directed by a Marxist-Leninist party.

"3. The revolutionary movement in every country must be in close touch with the international proletariat."

In the spring of 1927 Chiang Kai-shek, in order to win the support of conservative domestic landlords, bankers, and warlords and the neutrality of the western nations and their commercial interests in China for his campaign to unify that unhappy nation, suddenly and unexpectedly turned on his Communist allies. Thousands of Chinese Communists were slaughtered in Canton and other cities, their Party broken up and driven underground (a few remnants, led by Mao Tse-tung, took to the mountains), and all ties with the Soviet Union cut. Ho Chi Minh's Thanh Nien group suffered along with their Chinese comrades, but the leaders, including Ho, escaped. At the end of 1927 Ho Chi Minh left for Moscow and then made a tour of European capitals—Brussels, Paris, Bern, Berlin and Rome—where he established contacts with the revolutionary and Communist parties. But by November 1928 he was back in the Far East, this time in northeastern Siam. There, disguised as a Buddhist monk, he opened another school for revolution, then moved on to Bangkok and established revolutionary cells within the pagodas, training the young bonzes (Buddhist monks) in social philosophy.

It was during this odd phase of Ho's life that events in Indochina made the establishment of a Communist Party there both possible and desirable. These events were a series of strikes in the mines, the factories, the rubber plantations and the public transport systems, which underscored the fact that French industrialization had at last produced a large nucleus of urban working-class masses to whom such a Party might appeal. Previously, as we have seen, Ho had purposely soft-pedaled the Communist line in his dealings with Vietnamese followers in order to win the broadest possible support. But in his absence, the leadership of Thanh Nien (now operating in exile in British Hong Kong) split on this question and eventually established no fewer than three different Vietnamese Communist Parties. The resulting chaos in the Vietnamese revolutionary movement was only ended in February 1930, when, in response to pleas from his followers, Ho went to Hong Kong. There he summoned two representatives each from the three Communist groups and, during a soccer game at Hong Kong Stadium, ordered them to join together. The union was completed that same month and the official Indochinese Communist Party established. It immediately published a manifesto summing up its aims in ten points:

"1. To overthrow French imperialism, feudalism and the reactionary Vietnamese capitalist class.

"2. To make Indochina completely independent.

"3. To establish a government composed of workers, peasants and soldiers.

"4. To confiscate the banks and other enterprises belonging to the imperialists and put them under the control of the government.

"5. To confiscate the whole of the plantations and property belonging to the imperialists and the Vietnamese reactionary capitalist class and distribute them to poor peasants.

"6. To implement the eight-hour working day.

"7. To abolish public loans and the poll tax; to waive unjust taxes hitting the poor people.

"8. To bring back all freedoms to the masses.

"9. To carry out universal education.

"10. To implement equality between man and woman."

If these aims seem moderate for a Communist Party manifesto, they were so intended. Ho Chi Minh, in strict Marxist orthodoxy, still saw the Vietnamese revolution as going through three phases: (1) the expulsion of the French, for which all Vietnamese not utterly bound to the foreign conquerors must work; (2) the establishment of a middle-class democratic republic; and (3) the establishment of a socialist society. There seemed to be no way to short-circuit this lengthy process, but Ho, forty years old in 1930, was a patient man.

But the Vietnamese masses had lost patience. In 1930 the native troops of the garrison at Yen Bay mutinied and killed their officers. The mutiny was to have been the signal for a general uprising, but none occurred. The French Air Force bombed and strafed Yen Bay; French troops quickly put down the mutiny and many of its leaders were guillotined. Later that same year, in Ho's home province of Nghe-Trinh, the impoverished peasants and workers rose en masse and set up local soviets (in Russian the word means "councils") which, in a burst of nationalism, they labeled Xo-Viets. It is unclear what part Ho's Indochinese Communist Party played in this seemingly "spontaneous" movement, but the surprising organizational ability of the masses indicates that his lieutenants must have been very active. On September 12, 1930, about six thousand starving peasants staged a hunger march on the local city of Vinh. The French responded to these events with unbelievably cruel repressions. Literally thousands of men, women and children were slaughtered—sometimes after appallingly vicious torture—and the Nghe-Trinh Xo-Viets were suppressed. Officials of the Indochinese Communist Party's heirs in North Vietnam insist to this day that local Communist leaders were pushed much further than they had intended to go by the popular masses in Nghe-Trinh; in any event, this premature and ill-conceived uprising was to cost them dearly.

The French surété in Indochina rounded up many of Ho's followers. Some were tortured to death; others were sent to the infernal penal colony on the island of Poulo Condor, where many subsequently perished. Ho himself was still in Hong Kong, but he had been sentenced to death in absentia by a French court, and at the request of French authorities the British police arrested and imprisoned him. The French wanted them to extradite Ho back to Indochina immediately where certain death awaited him.

It was at this crucial moment that Ho Chi Minh's international contacts, the friendships he had established all over the world with leading revolutionaries and socialists, revealed their value.

Various international groups, some Communist dominated, some not, organized widespread protests demanding that Britain abide by the international right of political asylum and not "deliver the Indochinese patriots into the hands of the French torturers." An able and energetic English lawyer named Frank Loseby argued with various government leaders, who in turn carried the case to the Privy Council in London. Would the British government abide by its traditional policy of providing asylum for political exiles, or would it risk offending its French ally? In the end it did neither. Ho simply vanished from the Hong Kong jail, and his death was officially reported to the French authorities. Actually Ho was smuggled out of the prison hospital by Frank Loseby in July 1932, put aboard a boat to Amoy and told to lie low for a while. That all this was done with the connivance of the British authorities in Hong Kong seems indisputable and must be attributed to the powerful pressure brought to bear upon them by domestic political forces.

Ho's period of "lying low" did not last long. Within six months he turned up in Shanghai, where despite Chiang Kai-shek's spies and police agents he was able to get in touch with the Chinese Communist Party and also with the remnants of his followers in Indochina. But Shanghai soon became too dangerous a base. In 1933 Ho took a freighter to Vladivostok and then the Trans-Siberian railroad to Moscow. There he resumed his teaching role, this time at the Lenin Institute, where he lectured students in the Asiatic Department. The lectures were written in verse to "make study easier." In 1935 Ho attended the Seventh Congress of the Communist International and wholeheartedly supported its new and dramatic about-face, the creation of international "Popular Fronts."

For by 1935 the menace of Nazi Germany and Fascist Italy in Europe and militaristic Japan in the Far East overrode all other considerations in the mind of Soviet dictator Joseph Stalin. Alone, Russia could not withstand the all but inevitable onslaught of these three powers; she needed allies. To win them meant abandoning, for the time being, international Communist revolutionary agitation and substituting for it a policy of cooperation with any and all groups and governments throughout the world who would oppose fascism.

The fruits of this new policy were soon apparent in the relations between France and her Indochinese colony. In June 1936 the French Popular Front Government of Leon Blum (a broadly based coalition of French leftist groups with Communist support) sent a Commission of Inquiry to Indochina. A general amnesty for political prisoners was proclaimed, and many of Ho's surviving followers were released from prison. The Indochinese Communist Party was granted legal status as an Indochinese political party—and promptly won several local elections. On May 1, 1938, a joint demonstration called out by Indochinese Socialists and Communists brought tens of thousands of workers together, French and Vietnamese alike, to march through the streets of Hanoi.

All during this period of legal Popular Front political activity Ho Chi Minh remained in Russia, teaching and studying and being treated for tuberculosis, a malady that plagued him most of his life. But these peaceful years came to an end in 1938 when he returned to China. The Japanese invasion of that country had compelled Chiang Kai-shek to re-ally himself with Mao Tse-tung's Communists, now, after their incredible "Long March," firmly esconced in the hills of Yenan in the northern Chinese province of Shensi. There was nothing, then, to prevent Ho from visiting Mao Tse-tung, and he soon trekked north, pushing a small wheeled cart ahead of him in which he carried all his belongings. In Yenan Ho was appointed a political commissar to educate and indoctrinate Chinese troops in the principles of guerrilla warfare. And it was while he was in Yenan that World War II broke out in Europe—with immediate and eventual consequences to Vietnam of earth-shaking proportions.

The Thunderchief Goes Down

ON AUGUST 8, 1966, Major James Kasler, USAF, took part in a raid against railroad bridges and oil-storage facilities about fifty-five miles northwest of Hanoi. To Major Kasler, possibly the most renowned American pilot of the war in Vietnam, the target area was very familiar. Flying his Republic Aviation F-105 "Thunderchief" (armed with a 20mm. cannon firing 6,000 rounds per minute, capable of carrying additional fuel tanks to increase its range plus six 750-pound fragmentation bombs or the equivalent in napalm), Major Kasler had intruded into the skies above North Vietnam dozens of times. His squadron was part of the United States Tactical Air Command, which flew from bases in supposedly neutral Thailand—bases which, at that time, the United States government denied existed.

Major Kasler and his fellow pilots have described the antiaircraft defenses of the region around the Red River delta near Hanoi and Haiphong as the most concentrated and the deadliest in the world. Key targets are protected by radar-controlled antiaircraft guns ranging from 37mm. to 100mm. So heavy at times

60

THE THUNDERCHIEF GOES DOWN

THE THUNDERCHIEF GOES DOWN   61

has been the pattern of exploding antiaircraft shells over a target that passing through the "flak deck" has been likened to diving through a cloud. Especially important targets are also protected by numerous nests of Russian SAM ground-to-air missiles that seek out enemy planes and can destroy them simply by exploding nearby. When North Vietnamese Army units are in a target area they add their machine gun, rifle and mortar fire to the steel sleet storm through which attacking planes must pass. And there is always the possibility that North Vietnamese Air Force MiG-21 fighter planes will intervene. As many as six F-105s have been lost to these defenses on a single day of combat. And because of this heavy concentration of firepower, an American pilot shot down over the Red River delta has small prospects of being rescued.

Major Kasler, however, was not a man to be deterred from a mission. He had been an ace (shooting down six MiGs) in the Korean War and had volunteered energetically for combat in Vietnam. He was noted for his aggressiveness in getting close to a target; 3,500 feet was his preferred bombing altitude, although most F-105 pilots were content to release their bombs from 12,000 feet. Furthermore, after attacking his primary targets, Major Kasler was fond of expending his 20mm. cannon rounds on secondary "targets of opportunity." He had been reprimanded by General Momeyer (head of all American airpower in Southeast Asia) himself for taking needless risks. But Major Kasler had replied that once having passed over the antiaircraft defenses in the north, it seemed a waste of effort not to expend *all* his ammunition. Major Kasler's fighter bombers had sustained more than a few hits by antiaircraft shells, yet he always managed to bring them back to base. His reputation was such that his fellow pilots referred to him as *the* Thunderchief.

The mission of August 8, 1966, was Major Kasler's seventy-fifth of the war (after one hundred missions north of the Demilitarized Zone he would be rotated back to the United States)—and his last. After bombing the targets, Major Kasler's wingman was hit, ejected from his burning aircraft and parachuted to the ground. Since Major Kasler was low on fuel, he made a quick trip to the giant KC-135 tanker plane circling nearby, refueled and then hurried back to the spot where his wingman had gone down. He

The Thunderchiefs roar in.

began flying circles low over the area, hoping to catch a glimpse of the downed pilot. It was then that Major Kasler's plane took a hit from a heavy antiaircraft shell and began disintegrating. Major Kasler ejected and parachuted to the ground. Other F-105s in the area heard him radio that his leg was broken. Then his "beeper"— a radio homing device designed to guide rescue helicopters— began to function loud and clear. Although he was deep in enemy territory, there was still a slight chance that he might be rescued.

When General Momeyer, at his headquarters at Tan Son Nhut airfield near Saigon, received the news that Major Kasler was down he issued a clear and immediate order: "I want Major Kasler back! I don't care how many planes it takes. Now get going!"

Within minutes, from secret forward bases, Sikorsky HH-3C helicopters—dubbed "Jolly Green Giants" and especially equipped for rescue missions—muttered aloft to make their dangerously slow way through the hail of antiaircraft fire to the Red River. To escort them and to suppress enemy ground fire against the vulnerable "choppers," dozens of slow prop-driven Douglas A-1 Skyraiders went along. But since both the Jolly Green Giants and the Skyraiders would make easy targets for North Vietnamese MiG jets, an additional force of McDonnell F-4 Phantom jet fighters were ordered to fly "cover" to the entire mission—to pounce on any MiGs that might appear. And since this huge force of planes would need fuel, additional KC-135 air tankers were ordered to circle the area. To make sure that all this activity was coordinated, a Lockheed C-130 Hercules flying command post was dispatched. And, finally, the pilots of Major Kasler's F-105 squadron were given permission to fly in from Thailand to search for their chief.

Soon the sky over Major Kasler's bail-out position was so thick with planes of all descriptions that the thunder of their engines could be heard for many miles. Air collisions were averted by a miracle. But though the Jolly Green Giants hovered low over the ground searching desperately, they could catch no glimpse of the major. Then his "beeper" fell silent—and it was apparent that Major Kasler's war was over.

But although the indestructible Thunderchief's fighting days were ended, he himself was not. A few weeks after he was shot down, American television screens displayed a newsreel taken in Hanoi, showing North Vietnamese surgeons operating on Major Kasler's broken leg. He remains a prisoner of war in North Vietnam, his life preserved by those enemies he attacked so determinedly.

Chapter Four

PATHS TO VICTORY

> All men are created equal. They are endowed by their Creator with certain unalienable rights; among these are Life, Liberty and the pursuit of Happiness.
> —*The Vietnamese Declaration of Independence, September 2, 1945*

THE INDOCHINESE Communist Party, though recognized as legal by the French colonial administration, began going underground in late 1938. Whether this was done on Ho Chi Minh's instructions from China or on the initiative of local leaders is impossible to determine. Likewise, it is difficult to imagine what "inside" information or extrasensory perception led the ICP to take this step. Had Ho any advance notice that Russian dictator Joseph Stalin would, in the not distant future, sign that infamous Treaty of Mutual Aid and Friendship with Hitler's Germany which brought the entire Popular Front down with a crash? Or, as was more likely, did the ICP go underground on the basis of a general suspicion of French authorities? In any event, this timely action undoubtedly saved the lives of many ICP leaders.

With the signing of the Soviet Russian-Nazi German Non-Aggression Pact in August 1939, Communist Parties dutifully shifted their lines from vivid anti-fascism to uncertain neutralism. The western democracies now justifiably regarded their domestic Communist Parties as real or potential subversive allies of Nazi

German aggression. When Germany invaded Poland in September 1939, thereby plunging Europe into war, France and Britain took immediate steps to suppress Communist activity both at home and in their colonies.

To Indochina France sent a new governor general, the stern General Georges Catroux. Within days of his arrival thousands of Indochinese Communist Party members were arrested and shipped off to Poulo Condor. The Party organization and all its apparatus was effectively smashed. But because of their foresight, many of the Party's leaders were able to flee across the border into southern China.

But General Catroux's administration did not last long. In the spring of 1940 Hitler's mechanized hordes smashed through French resistance in Europe and brought the Third French Republic to an end. Aged Marshal Henri Pétain now set up his reactionary French vassal state with its capital at Vichy and followed a policy of subservience to the German conquerors. To make sure that the policy of the colonial authorities in distant Indochina conformed to that of Vichy, Marshal Pétain replaced General Catroux as governor general with Admiral Jean Decoux. The admiral's administration could barely maintain itself with the forces available—primarily a few units of the French Foreign Legion and a few battalions of native troops. The French fleet was out of action; reinforcements and supplies could not be expected from metropolitan France. So when the Japanese, in September 1940, demanded that they be allowed to establish bases in Indochina for their endless war against China, both the Vichy government and the colonial administration in Saigon could only agree. Japanese forces soon began flooding into the colony. Their "bases" soon expanded to control entire provinces; by the middle of 1941 they had established control over Indochina's rice and rubber exports through a series of agreements forced down French throats. With Japanese connivance, Siam attacked Indochina in March 1941 and won parts of Laos and Cambodia. In July 1941 Japanese forces occupied southern Indochina—from which area, in December 1941, they launched attacks against Malaya, Siam, the Dutch East Indies and the Philippine Islands, thereby extending World War II to the Far East.

It might be well to note here that with their sudden and extremely successful offensives of late 1941 and early 1942, the Japanese very effectively demonstrated the strategic value of Indochina as a springboard to the domination of all Southeast Asia and the islands down to Australia. Naval and air forces based on Indochina could completely sever lines of communication and supply throughout the area—and dominate the waters of the South China Sea. If the success of the Japanese surprise attack against the mighty American bastion at Pearl Harbor produced something of a traumatic shock among American military leaders and the American people—leading to the post-World War II determination that such an event must never happen again; that the state of American military preparedness must hereafter remain high—the effectiveness of Indochina as a Japanese base of operations made its own deep impression on American minds. Especially in military circles, the belief took root that the United States could never again afford to see Indochina fall into potential

Soldiers of the Rising Sun pedal south into Indochina; their ultimate destination, World War II.

enemy hands. And while military strategy and tactics might be revolutionized in the decades following World War II, this theory retained its tenacious hold on American military thinking—with profoundly tragic results.

While the Japanese used Indochina as a great base and staging area for their offensives and took over effective control of the colony's economy as well as many aspects of its government, they nonetheless permitted Admiral Decoux's regime to maintain its formal status. After all, Vichy France was an ally of Japan's ally, Nazi Germany—and besides, the French in Indochina made useful administrators, while they posed no threat to Japanese control. In effect, the Japanese were using the French in much the same way that the French had used the mandarins in days gone by—an irony not lost on the Vietnamese people.

The Japanese domination of Indochina only served to increase the burdens under which the Vietnamese people staggered. Although the new intruders proclaimed a policy of "Asia for the Asiatics" and talked much of their "Greater East Asia Co-Prosperity Sphere," it was soon apparent that the Japanese were intent only on the ruthless exploitation of all subject peoples. Their presence in Indochina added new fuel to Vietnamese nationalism. It also made the suppressed Vietnamese automatically allies of China, Britain and the United States, as well as other Asiatic peoples, in the common struggle against Japan.

But even before the Japanese struck out at wider objectives in the Far East, Ho Chi Minh and the handful of Vietnamese Communist leaders who had escaped the French repression of 1939 began planning their expulsion from Indochina. At this time (the summer of 1940) Ho himself was still working as a political instructor to certain units of Chiang Kai-shek's Nationalist Army. Fleeing from both the French and the Japanese, two men now came to him who would become his most trusted disciples: Pham Van Dong and Vo Nguyen Giap. To them Ho preached his new strategy for Vietnamese independence. The time for a general insurrection was not yet at hand, Ho maintained (and the abortive uprisings in Indochina during the fall of 1940 confirmed this); what was needed was the immediate organization of the most broadly based resistance movement, one that would incor-

porate all Vietnamese who wanted to see their country liberated,
regardless of their political outlook. Furthermore, this new Vietnamese liberation movement would have to ally itself with the
forces of Chiang Kai-shek. This was a practical necessity—Mao
Tse-tung's Communist armies were too far away in northern
China, and Allied power was for the moment expelled from East
Asia. Despite Chiang's known hatred of Communists and his suspected ambition to reassert Chinese sovereignty over Vietnam,
only his forces could supply the needed weapons and bases for
the struggle.

In the winter of 1940, perhaps copying Mao Tse-tung's successful tactics in Yenan, Ho and his followers set up a tiny
"liberated zone"—that of Pac Bo, in the northernmost area of
Tonkin, just south of the Chinese border. A few weeks later, at
the end of January 1941, Ho Chi Minh returned to his native land
after an absence of thirty years. He established his headquarters
in a large cave in the limestone hills near the village of Pac Bo.
From there he traveled through the region, passing out a small
newsletter called *Viet Lap* (Independent Vietnam) and instructing all who would listen in his revolutionary program.

It was in the cave of Pac Bo, from May 10 to May 19, 1941, that
Ho presided over the eighth meeting of the leadership of the
Indochinese Communist Party. At this meeting it was agreed that
a new national liberation movement must be established. Thus
was born one of the most famous organizations in recent history,
the League for Vietnamese Independence (Vietnam Doc Lap
Dong Minh)—or, for short, the Vietminh. Its objectives were
primarily nationalistic—the independence of the Vietnamese
people; its program was limited to one immediate objective:
"After the overthrow of the Japanese Fascists and French imperialists, a revolutionary government of the Democratic Republic of Vietnam will be set up in the spirit of the new democracy;
its emblem will be the red flag with a gold star." Only in the color
of its flag, then, did the Vietminh reveal its ultimate objectives.

Having set up the Vietminh, and with Vo Nguyen Giap's guerrilla bands already beginning to be active in the highlands of
Tonkin, Ho decided to make another trip to China. He felt the

need of further discussions with the Chinese Nationalists and also hoped to reestablish communications with Mao Tse-tung in the north. But no sooner had Ho crossed the border in July 1942 than he was arrested by soldiers of the Chinese Nationalist Marshal Chang Fa-kwei, a supporter of Chiang Kai-shek but something of a local warlord in his own right too. What had happened to bring about Ho's arrest? Had he not been counting on Chinese Nationalist support? Yes. But in his absence, the government of Chiang Kai-shek had thought long and hard about Indochina. After all, the colony had once been a Chinese province; perhaps it might become so again. The Chinese Nationalists had instructed Marshal Chang, who controlled the border area, to establish a Vietnamese Liberation Committee composed of Vietnamese who would follow Chinese instructions and perhaps eventually form a puppet government in Vietnam that would once again recognize Chinese overlordship. The nature of this committee was best illustrated by the fact that its head, an old Vietnamese nationalist named Nguyen Hai Than, had lived abroad for so long that he no longer could speak his native language! Obviously, it was against Chinese interests that a real Vietnamese liberation movement arise—hence the arrest of Ho Chi Minh.

In any event, Ho's imprisonment was a harsh experience. He was moved from jail to jail—marching barefoot down the roads, sometimes with a yoke over his shoulders, sometimes shackled to his fellow prisoners. The jails themselves were pestholes beyond description: one of the men to whom Ho was chained died one night huddled against him. Yet throughout this terrible time Ho Chi Minh found time to write poetry:

> *The rice-grain suffers under the pestle;*
> *yet admire its whiteness when the ordeal is over.*
> *It is the same with human beings in our time—*
> *to be a man, you must endure the pestle of misfortune.*

and:

> *The poems of our day must be clad in steel.*
> *Poets too must know how to fight!*

and:

> *. . . Being chained is a luxury to compete for.*
> *The chained have somewhere to sleep,*
> *the unchained haven't . . .*
> *The State treats me to its rice, I lodge in its palaces,*
> *its guards take turns escorting me.*
> *Really, the honor is too great . . .*

Why did the Chinese Nationalists not seize this opportunity to kill Ho Chi Minh? For several possible reasons. First of all, by now Soviet Russia was part of the great alliance that had been forged against Nazi Germany in Europe, and it was plain that once victory was won there, Russia would probably throw her weight against Japan in the Far East. As a notable member of the Communist International, Ho was not without friends in Moscow and elsewhere. Secondly, old Marshal Chang Fa-kwei was anything but a canny politician; it is doubtful that he ever really understood the importance of the prisoner he held. And finally, and of greatest importance, the Chinese Nationalists hoped to persuade Ho to cooperate with their own Vietnamese Liberation Committee. The aged and fumbling Nguyen Hai Than had proved himself hopelessly incompetent; a new director was needed for the committee, a man who could count on real support in Indochina.

Pondering his position, Ho Chi Minh decided on a daring step. He told Marshal Chang that he saw things "more clearly" now and would indeed cooperate with the Chinese-sponsored Liberation Committee. In so doing he risked not only eventual Chinese wrath but, more immediately, the loss of all his supporters in the Vietminh who might not understand this sudden apparent "betrayal." Nonetheless, he accepted the risks, and in the spring of 1943 Ho Chi Minh, the militant Communist, the leader of the radical Vietminh, the acknowledged head of the Vietnamese nationalistic movement, found himself director of the Chinese puppet Liberation Committee, being supported by Chiang Kai-shek to the tunc of $100,000 per month!

As soon as he could, Ho made a trip to Indochina to explain his motives to his Vietminh followers. The day of Allied victory in both Europe and the Far East was now in sight. The time had come for the Vietminh to begin active and widespread military operations against the Japanese and the French. For this they needed Chiang's money—and they also needed contact with the British and the Americans who were now closing in on the crumbling Japanese Empire. All of this could be had only through the infiltration and manipulation of the phony Chinese-sponsored Liberation Committee. The Vietminh understood. By this time, in any event, so great was Ho's reputation among all Vietnamese, so revered was he as the founder and leader of the Vietnamese independence movement, that his followers would probably have trusted him to make a pact with the devil himself.

But while the newly vitalized Vietminh, largely under Giap, who was developing into something of a military genius, began to spread their guerrilla activities against the Japanese throughout ever larger areas of Tonkin, changes were taking place in the relationship between Indochina and France—or so Ho and his followers hoped.

When France had fallen before Nazi German might in 1940, not all Frenchmen had surrendered. Many had fled to London to continue the struggle from there. They were headed by General Charles de Gaulle, a fervent French patriot and nationalist. A struggle soon developed between the Gaullists in London and the representatives of the puppet government of Marshal Pétain in Vichy for control of the French colonies overseas. These were often strategically situated so as to be of very great importance in the war plans of Britain and the United States. De Gaulle, as head of the "Fighting French," enjoyed the support of England and, grudgingly, of the Americans. United States policy, developed by President Franklin D. Roosevelt, Secretary of State Cordell Hull and other U. S. administration leaders, was very definitely anti-colonial. Roosevelt in particular thought that after the war Britain and France should retire from their colonies and allow them to seek independence and nationhood. That, he thought, would contribute to a more peaceful and settled postwar world. If American blood and treasure were to be spent in the great global war against fascism, it was not to re-create worldwide imperialism. British Prime Minister Winston Churchill, on the other hand, had no intention, as he once said, of "presiding over the liquidation of the British Empire."

From this conflict of views grew a strange and confused policy. Both England and the United States were more or less forced to support General de Gaulle, as the only viable alternative to the pro-Fascist regime of Marshal Pétain in France. Furthermore, for strategic reasons they had to support General de Gaulle's right to rule the former French colonies. But while Roosevelt and the Americans planned to do everything possible to ensure the liberation of as much as possible of France's prewar overseas empire, Churchill and the British were forced, as a matter of principle, to support French claims to the French Empire—how else could they in good conscience reclaim their own? As far as French Indochina was concerned, then, both Britain and the United States supported Gaullist efforts to undermine the rule of Vichy's Admiral Decoux as part of the general war effort against Japan. But the United States was not eager to see Indochina liberated by French forces, for that would mean the reestablishment of the prewar French colonial regime in Hanoi.

At first, Ho Chi Minh and his followers hoped that the advent of De Gaulle might herald a new French policy toward Indochina. After all, De Gaulle was an ally in the war against fascism (and imperialism was but one form of fascism)—and De Gaulle depended absolutely on American supplies and money. But on December 8, 1943, in the recently liberated French colony of Algeria, General de Gaulle spoke of France's "need" to reestablish her authority in Indochina. Evidently not even the defeat of Japan and of the Vichy colonial regime of Admiral Decoux would bring about Vietnamese independence. In fact, representatives of De Gaulle and of Admiral Decoux met in China, where they agreed on at least one thing: no matter how the war ended, France would maintain herself in her great Southeast Asian colony.

Vietminh policy now underwent a rapid change. Evidently it was not possible to ally with the French in a common cause against the Japanese. The broadly based appeals to patriotism were now misleading. From now on Vietminh propaganda insisted on a twofold struggle: against the Japanese, and equally against the French in Indochina. Guerrilla warfare now aimed not only to liberate areas from Japanese control, but also to prepare the way for a general insurrection against French rule, whether personified by Admiral Decoux or by the representatives of General de Gaulle. The French responded by asking the Chinese Nationalists to cease giving support to the Vietnamese insurrectionists. This request was not granted, however, since it was through the Vietnamese insurrectionists that the Chinese imagined they might reestablish their own overlordship over Indochina.

Meanwhile, the guerrilla activities of Giap's men met with greater and greater success. Ho and the Vietminh leadership were soon able to move out of their Pac Bo base area to the foothills and mountains farther south. Sometimes the Vietminh guerrillas were supported by French troops who had deserted the Vichy colonial regime of Admiral Decoux and would join anyone fighting the Japanese. Village after village fell into Vietminh hands; sometimes entire garrisons of Vietnamese soldiers in French employ went over to the Vietminh cause. By the beginning of 1945 Vietminh strength was such that the French authorities in Hanoi decided to act.

Admiral Decoux's military advisors devised a comprehensive plan to wipe out the Vietminh. Officers and men were chosen to lead a "mopping-up" expedition to the Tonkinese highlands. The French forces at hand seemed more than adequate to deal with Ho's guerrillas, and March 12, 1945, was chosen as the expedition's jumping-off date. But three days before, on March 9, 1945, the Japanese forces in Indochina struck.

Ever since 1940 the Japanese, while holding the real power in Indochina, had been content to allow Admiral Decoux and his followers the illusion of governing. But now, with American fleets bombarding Japanese coastal cities, with American soldiers preparing for the final assault against the Japanese home islands, it seemed to Japan's militarist government that only a decisive drive on China could win the territory they would need for bargaining at the peace table. Not only that, but by launching a reinvigorated front against southern China they hoped to win the airfields from which American B-29 bombers were flying daily to grind Japan's cities to rubble. This all-out effort demanded complete control of the base area of Indochina. The time had arrived for Admiral

Decoux's sham government to be wiped out. Accordingly, Japanese units throughout Indochina fell upon the unsuspecting French garrison forces and either killed or imprisoned them. French rule in Indochina was ended overnight.

In a way, all of this proved a godsend to Ho. The Japanese were far less experienced and skillful in dealing with the Vietnamese insurrectionists than were the French. Furthermore, with the Vichy administration of Decoux now out of the way, the fighting lines were drawn much more clearly. While certain ragtag French forces who had escaped the Japanese carried on guerrilla warfare against them, the prime resistance to Japan in Indochina was now clearly the Vietminh. This meant that the Vietminh were entitled to Allied support. To show their strength, Giap's guerrillas continued their southward advance and soon amalgamated several liberated areas into a so-called free zone that included a remarkably large region in the Tonkinese highlands.

In February 1945—even before the Japanese struck—Ho Chi Minh had journeyed to Kunming in China to meet the American military mission stationed there. While the Americans were well aware that Ho's movement was Communist, they were eager to help him—both to make trouble for the Japanese and to ensure that the French would not reestablish themselves in Indochina. Accordingly, the U.S. Office of Strategic Services (OSS) men in Kunming supplied Ho's guerrillas with a substantial quantity of light arms and ammunition. Evidently, from accounts published years later, Ho himself made a very favorable impression on the Americans. One of them recalled: "Ho was an awfully sweet guy. . . . If I had to recall one quality of this old man sitting on his hill in the jungle, it would be sweetness. . . ."

In July 1945 further contacts were made with the Americans, and through them a document (in English) outlining the Vietminh's political aims was passed on to General de Gaulle's representatives in China. The aims stated in this paper were remarkably moderate; in fact, independence for Vietnam was to be achieved in not "less than five years nor more than ten." The French mission in China, lacking instructions from their home government in Paris, were obliged to return a noncommittal reply, though a very courteous one. In fact the French government had already issued a statement of its policy in Indochina, and the dominant theme of that statement had been that the colony was to remain divided into its prewar constituents: Tonkin, Annam, Cochin China, Cambodia and Laos. Furthermore, the Annamese French puppet emperor, Bao Dai, who had cooperated with the Japanese, would be the nominal head of the new Indochina. Of course this statement of French policy was known to Ho Chi Minh. Why, then, did he treat the French mission in China with such equanimity? For two main reasons.

First of all, there was no need to alert the French to the real Vietminh aims, or, more particularly, to the real Vietminh strength and determination. While still struggling against the Japanese, Ho Chi Minh had no desire to find himself attacked by even the ragged French forces wandering the jungles of Indochina. Secondly, it was at about this time that Ho learned of the Allies' plans for the Chinese Nationalist armies of Chiang Kai-shek to occupy northern Indochina. This plan had two roots in American thinking. First, when Japan collapsed no American forces would be available to occupy Indochina, and it would be advantageous to use Chinese troops. Secondly, the presence of Chinese troops under American auspices in Indochina would preclude any French attempt to reoccupy the colony. Of course this plan had been devised before the Americans became aware of the very real strength of the Vietminh in Indochina, which had now developed into a force potentially able to fulfill all the roles hoped for from the Chinese. But plans once made, agreements entered into are not easy to change. For his part Chiang Kai-shek, seeing this legal occupation of northern Indochina as part of his undercover effort to regain the area for China, was not disposed to give it up. Aware of all this, Ho had come to the conclusion that the Vietminh might well need French cooperation to prevent a Chinese take-over. Hence his desire to appear as cooperative as possible to Paris.

If all of this seems somewhat complicated to us, it might be well to remember that it seemed straightforward to Ho and the Vietminh. It was simply a policy of isolating and identifying one's major and most dangerous enemy at any given time. Presently it was Japan; later it would be the Chinese Nationalists; still later it would be the returning French; much later it would become the imperialist Americans. At any given stage of developments, one could ally oneself with any of these forces to drive out any other. In the summer of 1945, despite the troubles already so apparent on the horizon, the Vietminh, the French and the Americans—and even the Chinese Nationalists—were supposedly united to destroy the Japanese.

This destruction made rapid progress during the late summer of 1945. Ho Chi Minh's advisors, especially the enthusiastic General Giap, urged him to call for a general uprising against the Japanese. That way the Vietminh could seize power in Indochina before the French had a chance to return. But Ho, although aware that Japan faced imminent defeat in the Pacific, realized that the Japanese occupation armies in Indochina were too strong; an insurrection would only lead to the slaughter of thousands of Vietnamese. Therefore he bided his time. Only when news came of the atomic bombing of Hiroshima on August 6, 1945, did Ho call for decisive action, and it was not until August 15, 1945 (one day *after* the Japanese surrender to the Allies), that the Vietminh in Hanoi were permitted to rise.

On August 16, 17, 18 and 19, Vietminh elements throughout Indochina came out into the open. Great mass demonstrations involving hundreds of thousands of people took place in Hanoi, Hué and Saigon. The countryside blossomed with Vietminh flags. On August 25, 1946, Vietminh representatives forced the abdication of the imperial government of Bao Dai—and by that day they had won control of all Indochina.

What of the Japanese forces still in Indochina, awaiting repatriation to their defeated homeland? They simply looked the other way. If Japan was not to have Indochina, neither, at least, were the French. It must have been with some ironic amusement that the Japanese in Indochina watched the Vietminh take over the country. As for the French, their representatives in China could not seem to get to Hanoi, because the United States commander in China, General Wedemeyer, could not find transportation for them! It would seem then that the Vietminh uprising had at least the tacit support of the Americans. It was all very remarkable—but bear in mind that these were tearfully exciting days for the men who, led by Ho Chi Minh, had fought for decades to liberate their homeland.

On August 29 a new government was announced by the Vietminh in Hanoi (to which city Ho had returned on August 21), with Ho Chi Minh as president of the Democratic Republic of Vietnam. A few days later the Vietnamese Declaration of Independence was issued, with its ringing reaffirmation of the rights of man copied from the American original. And later that month President Ho Chi Minh wrote two open letters to his people. To the youth of his country:

"My children,
"Today we start the first term of the Democratic Republic of Vietnam. . . . Eighty years of slavery have diminished our country's strength. Now we must retrieve the heritage bequeathed by our ancestors and catch up with the other nations of the world. . . ."

And to the old people of his country:

"Gentlemen,
"It is as an old man that I address you . . ."

CLOSE-UP

The Fate of Nam Dinh

ON APRIL 29, on May 19 and again on June 1, 1966, the United States Military Briefing Officer in Saigon informed American correspondents that the North Vietnamese city of Nam Dinh had been bombed. The military targets involved were said to be a railroad and "naval facilities." On Christmas Day, 1966, *New York Times* reporter Harrison Salisbury visited Nam Dinh as a guest of the North Vietnamese government. This is what he reported:

"We came into Nam Dinh from the north, and almost all the streets we drove through bore signs of bomb damage. . . .

"Two local officials briefed me about Nam Dinh, and from them I learned that it was a textile city of about ninety thousand people before most of them had been evacuated. They said Nam Dinh had been repeatedly subjected to United States attack—fifty-one or fifty-two raids up to that moment, including four on December 23. There had been, I was told, American reconnaissance planes over the city during the night, and thus far on Christmas morning the alert had sounded twice. . . .

What Harrison Salisbury saw at Nam Dinh.

"According to the inhabitants of Nam Dinh, the first serious raid on their city occurred June 28, 1965. This was carried out by two F-105s and two F-4Hs, they said, and took place about 7:30 on a cloudy morning. Two bullpup missiles had been fired into the area of the textile plant, they asserted, and ten persons, including three children, had been killed and twelve wounded.

"Many attacks, they said, had occurred at night, although U.S. planes do not usually attack at night in the north, and on occasion as many as twenty-seven planes had participated.

"One of the worst attacks, I was told, had hit Hang Thao (Silk Street) at about 6:30 A.M., April 14. This was a heavily populated thoroughfare, and normally there were 17,680 people living in the quarter. However, because of evacuation, only 2,300 remained. The bombs fell just at the moment when factories were changing shifts, and 49 people were said to have been killed and

135 wounded. It was also asserted that 240 houses had been destroyed.

"Another bad attack was launched in Hoang Van Thu Street, the residents said, not far from Silk Street, on May 18. . . . At 11:04 A.M. two F-4H planes emerged from the clouds, according to the residents. It was raining and had been raining for some time. Water was deep in the streets and many shelters were overflowing. Eight bombs, they said, fell in the area in a south-to-north bombing run. People were unable to get into the shelters and some who did were drowned. There were 13 killed and 11 wounded in the attack, I was told.

"We drove about Nam Dinh, through the textile area, and stopped in Silk Street. For blocks and blocks I could see nothing but desolation. Residential housing, stores, all the buildings were destroyed, damaged or abandoned. I felt that I was walking through the city of a vanished civilization. . . .

"I saw one enterprise which seemed to be functioning at close to the normal rate. This was the rice mill. . . . Inside the mill I saw stacked beside almost every production post a rifle. Some were propped beside open windows. Each worker had his tin helmet and a first-aid kit. . . . At the sound of the air-raid sirens the workers would grab their rifles and take up posts at the windows and on the roof to fire back at the American planes. Those who had no guns went into the shelters. . . .

"As I walked through Silk Street and saw the battered tower of the cathedral with its strings of red pennants and its white star of Bethlehem mounted for Christmas, looking out over a sea of destruction, I could not help but think of other scenes of wartime desolation. . . .

"Now it had happened to another city, a remote city in a remote country, a city whose name meant nothing to practically anyone in the whole of the United States, a city so obscure that we would have to hunt for it on the map of a country whose name most of us could not pronounce.

"What earthly meaning could be extracted from this destruction? What military purpose was it serving?

"It was hard to comprehend as I sat in the air-raid shelter outside the Nam Dinh municipal headquarters talking with the

Mayor [Tran Thi Doan], a woman whose petite figure suggested an age much closer to twenty than forty. . . .

"A great deal of Nam Dinh, said Mayor Doan, had disappeared —probably 13 percent of the city's housing, residences for 12,464 people. Casualties had been, considering everything, remarkably low—only 89 killed and 405 wounded, she said. But, of course, she added, 80 percent of the city's population had been evacuated and not many more than fifteen thousand people remained in Nam Dinh. My impression that it was a ghost city was borne out by her statistics.

"Why had Nam Dinh been attacked so heavily and so often?

" 'The Americans think they can touch our hearts,' said Nguyen Tien Canh [a Municipal Councillor]."

Chapter Five

INTO THE QUAGMIRE

> Today it is a case of the grasshopper pitted
> against the elephant. But tomorrow the ele-
> phant will have its guts ripped out.
> —OLD VIETNAMESE PROVERB

THE NATION over which the Vietminh ruled now was fearfully
war-torn. The north had never produced enough rice to feed itself,
depending even in the best of times on imports from the south; as
the year 1945 drew to a close, famine stalked the land. During the
next twenty months, claim the Vietminh, two million people died
of starvation in Vietnam. The French put the figure at four hundred thousand; either number is tragic. One of the first acts of the
Vietminh government in Hanoi was to institute severe rationing
—and fasting every tenth day. In considering all the events of
1945–1946, it is essential to recall this backdrop of intense and
widespread suffering.

The assumption of power by Ho Chi Minh's forces, their declaration of independence, the tacit support of the Americans—
all these by no means clarified the relationship between the Vietminh and France. Just as Ho was being named president of the
new republic, the French Gaullist representatives from China
were arriving in Hanoi. They were led by Jean Sainteny, a man
perfectly familiar with conditions in Indochina, a son-in-law of a

former governor general of the colony. Furthermore, a French expeditionary force convoyed by a French fleet under the command of General Jean Leclerc was already on the high seas bound for Haiphong. Clearly, the future relationship between Vietnam and France would have to be rapidly defined if fighting was to be avoided.

There were other factors calling for speedy negotiations between Ho and Jean Sainteny. For one, the British were about to occupy Saigon, where they would presumably "maintain order" until French forces arrived. More ominously, Chinese divisions were even now preparing to enter from the north and occupy all of Vietnam down to the sixteenth parallel. As we have seen, these measures were decided upon by the Allies during the war and confirmed at the Potsdam Conference of Russia, England and the United States in July 1945. Ho realized that the Vietminh alone could not hope to resist a Chinese occupation (an occupation, be it remembered, which the Vietminh had every reason to suspect of being permanent). To force Chinese withdrawal it was essential that the new government come to some understanding with the French.

Jean Sainteny, on his part, understood very well that France's days of outright colonial domination in Indochina were past. To reestablish the old colonial rule, the French General Staff in Paris estimated, would require a force of no less than three hundred thousand men plus huge sea and air forces. All of this was far beyond French means in 1945. Furthermore, American opposition to a renewal of French colonialism was obvious, and without American permission no French activity of any kind could be undertaken in the Far East. As Sainteny met with Ho Chi Minh he must have wondered: Would the Americans eventually cooperate to persuade the Chinese to leave Indochina? Would the British in Saigon really turn the city over to the French, or would they, under American pressure, turn it over to the Vietminh? Above all, would the French government in Paris understand that Vietnamese independence was an accomplished fact—a fact that France would have to somehow recognize?

By December 1945 events were forcing Ho and Sainteny to reach speedy agreement. Chinese armies were already fanning out through the Red River delta; General Leclerc's forces had touched at Saigon (where, despite French suspicions, the British willingly turned over power to them) and were now sailing north. The issue of prime importance that separated the French and Vietnamese positions was simply what form French authority would now take in Indochina. The Paris government was willing to accept Vietnamese independence in the form of "home rule" by the Vietnamese, provided the new government in Hanoi would agree to enter an Indochinese Federation that was to include Cambodia and Laos, and to accept the creation of a separate state (within the Federation) of Cochin China. Ho Chi Minh, on the other hand, insisted that North and South Vietnam be considered one country (as indeed it was) and that Vietnam would not enter into any Indochinese Federation, but would consider itself an independent nation within the French Union; would accept, that is to say, something like the status of Canada within the British commonwealth of nations. Thus France might maintain some of the symbols and status of dominion, provided she recognized the integrity of the Vietnamese nation and its basic independence. Furthermore, Ho was very willing to reestablish close economic and cultural ties with France and to accept the presence of French armed forces at specified points in Vietnam—in much the same spirit that the Philippine government had accepted the presence of American forces at the naval base of Cavite.

While negotiations proceeded at a snail's pace between Ho and Sainteny, a general election was held throughout Vietnam. It produced a 97 percent majority for Ho and the Vietminh; nevertheless, Ho formed a coalition cabinet that included Vietnamese conservatives and nationalists as well as Communists.

On March 4, 1946, it was learned in Hanoi that General Leclerc's expeditionary force was already in the Gulf of Tonkin, approaching Haiphong. Only a few days earlier, the French had finally wrung an agreement from Nationalist China that Chinese troops would be withdrawn from Indochina when French forces arrived. To win this, France had been forced to relinquish all her pre-World War II special concessions, rights and privileges in Chinese coastal cities such as Canton, Shanghai and Tientsin and surrender her former leasehold of the Chinese territory of Kwang-chowan. In other words, France had given up all the imperialist gains she had won over the centuries in China in return for the right to repossess Indochina.

As the French fleet approached, Hanoi was gripped by war fever. Europeans went about desperately trying to buy pistols and rifles. They fully expected a Vietnamese rising and a general massacre to occur as soon as the first French soldier attempted to land. But at dawn on March 6, with French warships only a few miles outside Haiphong, Ho Chi Minh and Sainteny finally reached an accord. But even this last-minute agreement was almost wrecked by an unexpected crisis. For as the first French warships entered Haiphong harbor, at noon on March 6, they were fired upon by Chinese forces under the command of Chinese Nationalist General Gaston Wang. General Wang claimed he knew nothing of the Franco-Chinese agreement for Chinese withdrawal. After suffering more than a few casualties, the French fleet returned the Chinese fire, blowing up a large ammunition dump in Haiphong. At this the Chinese ceased firing, and French troops began disembarking peacefully.

Late on the same afternoon, Ho and Sainteny signed their formal agreement. The document declared that France would "recognize the Republic of Vietnam as a free state having its own government, parliament and its own finances, and forming part of the Indochinese Federation and the French Union." As for the future of Cochin China (southern Vietnam), the French agreed to abide by the decision of its local inhabitants in a special election to be held within a reasonably short time. Thus Ho was forced to accept the Indochinese Federation, and even the potential separation of Cochin China from Vietnam. Of course he had every reason to expect that the inhabitants of the south would vote overwhelmingly to join their northern brethren in one Vietnamese nation.

If Ho and his Vietminh followers could derive but little satisfaction from the agreement reached with Sainteny, the people of Hanoi and Haiphong, not fully comprehending the intricacies of the matter, were enraged. Was it for this—for the reestablishment of French authority (and no matter how disguised by words, that authority was painfully evident in the presence of those French soldiers and warships)—that they had fought for so long? Ho and his men were reviled as traitors; they had sold out to the enemy. So alarmed was the government by the hostile reaction to its agreement, that a huge mass meeting was called on March 7 in Hanoi. There, before more than one hundred thousand of their suspicious countrymen, Ho Chi Minh, Vo Nguyen Giap and other Vietminh leaders attempted to explain and justify their actions.

"I, Ho Chi Minh," the president's voice rang out, "have always led you along the path to freedom; I have spent my whole life fighting for our country's independence. You know I would sooner die than betray the nation. I swear I have not betrayed you!" Those closest to the president could see tears coursing down his cheeks. The impact of that simple statement was enough; with a tremendous roar of approval the crowd accepted Ho's policy.

It might be supposed that the French would be gratified by the agreement between Ho and Sainteny. As a matter of fact, when General Leclerc arrived in Hanoi on March 18 he was very obviously pleased both with the agreement and with Ho Chi Minh ("So, we meet at last as friends, Mister President," the general beamed as he shook hands with Ho). But the French high commissioner for Indochina, Admiral Thierry D'Argenlieu, who had remained in Saigon all this time, looked upon Ho, the Vietminh, the new Vietnamese nation and the agreement with bitter distaste. In this he reflected the opinions of a powerful conservative majority among French residents of Indochina and a highly nationalistic minority among the citizens of metropolitan France. Nevertheless, Admiral D'Argenlieu swallowed his disgust and even managed to maintain a polite atmosphere when he finally met Ho Chi Minh aboard the French crusier *Emile Berlin* in April.

For the French government was determined to implement the Ho-Sainteny agreement. And in order to do so they had invited Ho Chi Minh and a delegation from the Vietnamese parliament to visit Paris. There the final terms of Vietnam's new relationship to France were to be worked out in formal detail. Perhaps the French counted on Paris to stir old memories in Ho—memories of his many French radical friends, of that French culture in which the aged revolutionary still delighted. On May 30, 1946, Ho Chi Minh and his delegation boarded the plane for Paris. But while still airborne—flying over Damascus—he learned of a French betrayal.

Only a few hours after Ho had departed, Admiral D'Argenlieu had gone on the Saigon radio to announce the creation of a "Republic of Cochin China," a free and independent state within the Indochinese Federation and the French Union. This was a matter, it must be remembered, that Sainteny and Ho had agreed would be left for the people of Cochin China themselves to decide. True, the admiral had made reference to such a "referendum," but it was very apparent that the French intended to preempt the decision of the people and, most probably, "manipulate" any future vote on the subject.

Yet Ho's visit to France (he stayed first at Biarritz and then in Paris) was not utterly unproductive. It seemed, explained the French, that there had been a misunderstanding from the very beginning. From the first, France had understood that despite the coming referendum (which, Ho was assured, would certainly be held), the organization of Cochin China would proceed, pending a final decision by its people. In any event, with or without Cochin China, the new state of Vietnam would be remaining part of the overall Indochinese Federation—so why make such a fuss? Ho, on the other hand, made good use of the fact that his own position at home was threatened by extremist groups who felt he had already conceded too much. If France pressed him too hard, the aged president of Vietnam pointed out, they might yet find themselves dealing with someone far more radical, far less attached, through memory and friendship, to France.

It was, in fact, in the renewal of old personal attachments and the formation of new that Ho and his delegation spent much of their time in France. To the door of the Vietnamese visitors came a steady stream of French socialists and Communists, as well as visitors representing other liberation movements throughout the world.

By mid-July it was apparent that the formal Franco-Vietnamese negotiations being held at Fontainebleau had failed. Yet

Ho was reluctant to give up hope that France might yet make those few concessions he needed in order to return home with any prospects of permanent peace. By September a formal agreement had been worked out which, whatever its language, simply reaffirmed the previous Ho-Sainteny accords, leaving the question of Cochin China unanswered. In fact, in certain details this new agreement was even less satisfactory to the Vietnamese than had been the old one. Ho left France aboard the French sloop *Dumont D'Urville* on September 19, 1946, a deeply troubled man. Three months in France had produced no real progress, and his followers in Hanoi were pressing for action.

Some of them, indeed, had already taken action. Sporadic terrorist attacks, sometimes by the Vietminh, often by other nationalist groups, had been occurring for months in Cochin China. With Ho's return and the announcement of the terms of the agreement at Fontainebleau these terrorist activities spread to the north, to the new Vietnamese republic itself. Small bands of guerrillas would attack French outposts, seize French payrolls, shoot up French convoys. It is difficult to tell whether the Vietnamese government encouraged this activity, merely tolerated it, or actively tried to suppress it. Ho certainly seems to have waged a struggle to maintain peace during the weeks following his return. But General Giap, always more optimistic and perhaps more belligerent than his leader, seemed confident that if only his forces were permitted to strike, he would be able to "sweep the French out of Hanoi overnight." It is unlikely that, as commander of the Vietnamese armed forces, General Giap made any serious attempt to put down the continuing acts of "spontaneous" terrorism that steadily aggravated the French. And when a system of joint Vietnamese Militia–French Army military patrols was inaugurated to maintain order in Hanoi, Haiphong and the countryside, it was inevitable that misunderstandings and incidents within these patrols should further exacerbate the tempers of both sides.

Matters were brought to a head during the last week of November 1946. On November 20, concerned by reports of gunrunning from China, a French naval launch ordered a suspicious-looking Chinese junk to stop and be searched as it sailed into

Haiphong harbor. A nearby Vietnamese sentry immediately intervened—after all, Vietnam was supposed to be master of its own territorial waters and customs. When the French launch failed to heed his warnings, the Vietnamese sentry fired at it with his rifle. The launch immediately returned fire. Within a few hours barricades had gone up all over the city of Haiphong, from behind which Vietnamese Militiamen and French Army troops exchanged a hail of fire.

A joint French-Vietnamese commission succeeded in bringing about a cease-fire after a few hours, but the Vietnamese, fearing renewed French attack, refused to dismantle their barricades. A local French commander, Colonel Debes, ordered his men to sweep away the barricades at whatever cost and to "purge" the European quarters of the city of all Vietnamese, whether armed or not. French forces, who had sustained some casualties during the day, carried out this order ferociously. While Ho Chi Minh and French representatives in Hanoi desperately worked to reach some sort of accord that would avert total catastrophe, the French governor general in Saigon telegraphed Colonel Debes urging him to "exploit this serious incident to the full," and, later, "The time has come to give a harsh lesson to those who have attacked us. . . . By every means at your disposal, you must take control of Haiphong and bring the government and the Vietnamese Army to repentance. . . ."

On the morning of November 23, accordingly, Colonel Debes ordered that the Chinese quarter of Haiphong be cleared of Vietnamese forces by an armored column. When this force met with resistance he called for naval gunfire in support from the French cruiser *Suffren* lying in the harbor. The *Suffren's* gunners sighted on a distant line of figures which they mistook for a military unit. Actually it was a stream of refugees seeking to escape the carnage within the city. Heavy six-inch naval shells tore into this column and into various parts of Haiphong. More than six thousand Vietnamese were killed.

It appears that even in the face of this slaughter Ho Chi Minh still sought to find a basis for peaceful negotiations. His position had become all but impossible as his followers, especially the aggressive General Giap, pressed him to call for a national insur-

rection against the French. Incidents between French and Vietminh soldiers were now daily occurrences in Hanoi. Scores of
civilians perished amid sudden outbursts of gunfire. In Haiphong
Colonel Debes had finally cleared the entire city of Giap's men;
in Hanoi, as fast as the Vietminh dug trenches and erected
barricades, the French forces attacked them. It seemed apparent
that the French were using these last few days of negotiation only
to improve their military position.

The blow fell on December 19, 1946. At 8:30 P.M. a rumbling
explosion was heard in Hanoi, and suddenly the city was plunged
into darkness. The electric power stations had been blown up
by the Vietminh. Immediately, Vietminh forces opened fire
throughout the capital and fierce fighting raged for several hours.
But the French forces who had done so much to provoke this uprising were prepared for it. They immediately launched counter-
attacks against Vietminh strongholds, and Ho Chi Minh and the
Vietnamese government narrowly escaped capture by French
paratroopers. General Giap was not able, after all, to "sweep the
French" from Hanoi. Instead, he and his staff and his battered
troops retreated again into the mountain fastness of Tonkin.
There, under Ho Chi Minh's leadership, they established a "liberated zone" in which the Vietnamese government could function, and from this zone Vietminh guerrillas carried out incessant
hit-and-run attacks on French forces throughout Vietnam. After
sixteen months Ho and his men found themselves once again
operating as an outlawed armed underground within the nation
they had so briefly ruled. Ho issued a proclamation to his countrymen:

"Compatriots all over the country!

"As we desired peace, we made concessions. But the more we
made concessions, the further the French colonialists went, because they are resolved to invade our country once again.

"No! We would rather sacrifice all than lose our country. We
are determined not to be enslaved. . . .

"Those who have rifles will use their rifles; those who have
swords will use their swords; those who have no swords will use
spades, hoes, or sticks . . . victory will surely be ours!"

This proclamation marked the beginning of a long and bloody

war. It was a war in which the Vietminh were governed by the
three principles of guerrilla warfare laid down so long before by
the Chinese Communist leader Mao Tse-tung:

1. When the enemy attacks, we retreat.
2. When the enemy rests, we attack him.
3. When the enemy retreats, we pursue.

So the story of the next few years of uninterrupted and savage
conflict in Vietnam is not the story of any battles—except the last
—for no battles were really fought. Wherever the French Army
was able to maintain a large force, it ruled. Where it was unable to do so, the Vietminh ruled. Within a few weeks of the
opening of hostilities, the war settled into a pattern from which
it was not to emerge. The French occupied Hanoi, Haiphong,
Hué, Saigon and a few other large cities and their immediate
environs; the Vietminh controlled the countryside, the mountains and the jungles. French forces could not move anywhere in
Vietnam except in heavy military convoys, and even these were
sometimes successfully attacked. Terrorist activities took place
repeatedly—the blowing up of a French installation, the assassination of French officials—even in the heart of Hanoi and other
cities.

In order to maintain at least a French "presence" in areas
beyond the coastal cities, French forces fortified certain positions.
These were generally but not always secure from enemy attack.
On the other hand, the existence of these outposts gave the
Vietminh the opportunity to employ their favorite tactic, the
ambush. Fortified positions had to be supplied: supplies had to
be brought in by military convoy: convoys could be ambushed.
The classical Vietminh technique was simple, but terribly effective. Three bodies of troops would be deployed in the dense
jungles along a stretch of road. A French convoy would be permitted to pass down the road past the first two bodies of troops.
It was only when they reached the limit of the Vietminh deploy-
ment that they would be attacked from the sides and in front by
the third Vietminh force. Reacting, the French would attempt to
pull back along the road—only to find themselves attacked by the

middle Vietminh group, which cut off their line of retreat. This would cause the French to radio for reinforcements, but when these arrived they would be attacked by the first Vietminh force, which had waited patiently in the jungles for them. If sufficient French forces arrived to make the issue doubtful, the Vietminh would simply retire into the impenetrable jungles from which, like shadows, they had emerged.

The French never did discover any effective means of dealing with this ambushing technique. French air power was supreme in the skies above Indochina; the Vietminh had no planes and, until very late in the war, almost no antiaircraft weapons. But French air power was not massive during the 1950s, and in any event its effectiveness was strictly limited, because there simply were no Vietminh targets. Supply dumps and trails were heavily camouflaged in the dense undergrowth, very often hidden in deep caves; Vietminh soldiers almost never grouped together in any forces larger than a company unit or, on occasion, a battalion, and when

Where tanks could not maneuver, French forces had to resort to more ancient modes of transportation in pursuit of the Vietminh.

they did they were effectively protected by the natural cover of the local vegetation.

The primary story of the war waged between the Vietminh and the French for seven bloody years was political, and only through an understanding of its politics can its remarkable outcome be understood.

Ho Chi Minh's "war of the flea" against French imperial might followed a pattern made classical by the very long struggle between Mao Tse-tung's Chinese Communists and Chiang Kai-shek's Chinese Nationalist government. The strength of the Vietminh guerrillas was based on the fact that they emerged from and were an armed expression of the political views of the population of the areas in which they operated. Mao had said: "The people are the water, and we are the fish who swim in the water." Ho followed this policy exactly. Vietminh soldiers were, first of all, recruited from among local populations. They were trained in small groups in their own localities. They continued to live and to work among their fellow villagers when they were not fighting. When formed into groups and sent into combat in areas distant from their homes, they were instructed to treat their fellow peasants as if they were local friends and relatives. A Vietminh battalion was as adept at helping villagers plant or harvest their rice as it was in jungle warfare. Ho's shadow army really convinced almost all Vietnamese with whom it came into contact that it was indeed an expression of their will. And so it was.

For months that stretched into years, the strictly military side of operations was always subordinated to the political. Vietminh teachers, propagandists, and political commissars ceaselessly preached among the villagers and peasants their political philosophy in terms their audience could understand. They explained Vietminh aims and justified them. Needless to say, they were speaking to a very receptive audience—one that had experienced nearly a century of French repression. Success in this political warfare led to success in battle. From among the peasants came recruits; from them came food, information on enemy movements, and that moral support without which any army fights but poorly. And the peasants and villagers of Indochina offered refuge to the Vietminh whenever that was necessary too. It was only when the political campaign had been won in any given region that the Vietminh would undertake operations.

While waging this domestic political-military battle, Ho Chi Minh did not ignore the possibilities of foreign support. During the late 1940s it was becoming very apparent that the days of China's Nationalist regime were numbered. Mao Tse-tung's Communists were steadily advancing, and by 1948 their victory was in sight. Ho took every opportunity to renew his old ties with Mao, but not in such a way as might alarm either Russia's Communist government or, to a certain extent, the governments of England and the United States. Ho's war was, after all, at this stage, a war of liberation against colonial oppression. England was even then in the process of divesting itself of empire; the United States had all along been opposed to colonialism in Asia. Although the basic fact that Ho Chi Minh's Vietminh movement was Communist could not be hidden, Ho tried not to overly emphasize it. Vietminh appeals in the Communist world were addressed to "comrades"; in the capitalist world they were addressed to "all people of democratic, anti-colonialist views." While Ho could never hope to enlist massive public opinion on his side among the western nations, he sought to enlist enough of it to at least neutralize western support for the French. As we shall see, he was remarkably successful.

For the French, the political war in Vietnam was a continuous disaster on all fronts. In Indochina itself they could hope to enlist the support of only a fraction of the local population—precisely that fraction which, as middlemen between French masters and Vietnamese subjects, profited from French rule but in so doing earned themselves the hatred of their fellow Vietnamese. In an attempt to stir up support, the French government again turned to the former emperor of Annam, Bao Dai. He had been living in luxury amid the breath of scandals in Hong Kong and on the French Riviera. Now he was summoned to become emperor of all Vietnam. To win support for him among the Vietnamese, France gave to Bao Dai's Vietnam that which she would not surrender to Ho Chi Minh's government: Cochin China. Thus, on March 8, 1949, a new independent state of Vietnam, with Bao

Dai as emperor and including all of the country, came into being within the French Union. These were exactly the same terms Ho had agreed to but had been denied. The difference was apparent to all: Ho's Vietnam would have been a truly independent state with a government whose purpose was to revolutionize the nation's social structure so as to emancipate its people; Bao Dai's Vietnam was independent in name only—it was a puppet government subject to French will, one that was intent on preserving the status quo so as to protect French commercial interests in the country at whatever cost to its people. Although the French went so far as to create a separate Vietnamese Army under Bao Dai's government to help French forces fight the Vietminh, the emperor and his regime found no support among the Vietnamese people; Bao Dai's Vietnam remained a patent fraud supported only by French power.

Nor did French efforts to wage a propaganda war among the Vietnamese people make much progress. Since, in Vietnam, every hand might be raised against them, since they were fighting an enemy indistinguishable from the population itself, French tactics assumed a brutality that only earned them deeper hatred. Furthermore, since by French law no Frenchman could be drafted to fight overseas, French forces in Vietnam were composed of volunteers—the professional soldiers (of all nationalities) who composed France's Foreign Legion. These men were not noted for either discipline or tact, in dealing with native peoples. Soon the world would be nauseated by well-documented cases of torture, massacre and brutality perpetrated by French troops.

In France itself the endless campaign in Vietnam assumed larger and larger dimensions in domestic politics. The French Communist Party was extremely strong, and although uncertain at first as to what its relations with Ho Chi Minh's movement ought to be, it soon came out forcefully for French withdrawal from all its imperialist adventures—especially the bloody war in Vietnam. But French disgust at France's expensive and morally indefensible policy in Southeast Asia was not limited to French Communists; wider and wider segments of the French people grew first uneasy, then angry, then outraged at what was being done in their name. French governments had increasingly to take into account this steady shift in French public opinion.

Furthermore, on the level of international politics the French involvement in Vietnam assumed an ever more dangerous aspect. France was the ally of the United States and Britain, yet by continuing to wage war in Vietnam, France was increasingly risking the intervention against her of either Russia or China or both. This might well lead to incidents serious enough to provoke a third world war—and this was a catastrophe which no sane statesman, whether of the Communist or capitalist world, would welcome. Nor did the French campaign in Vietnam earn her the friendship of that "third world" of emerging underdeveloped nations that had themselves so recently escaped colonial bondage.

Thus, by the early 1950s, France found herself waging an endlessly expensive, endlessly bloody, endlessly demoralizing war against an enemy she could not defeat since she could never really come to grips with him. She found her own domestic politics growing increasingly bitter and divisive over this self-defeating war on the fringes of farthest Asia. She found herself also increasingly isolated among the nations of the world. France had plunged into the struggle to suppress the Vietminh like a man chasing a phantom into a swamp; now the man had fallen into quicksand and all his struggles seemed only to suck him further down. This was the quagmire indeed.

The War of the Knife

IN THE JUNE 8, 1964, issue of the magazine *U. S. News & World Report*, Robert L. Moore, Jr., a member of the United States Special Forces in Vietnam, replied to a lengthy series of interview questions:

Q. What's the job of Special Forces?

A. Special Forces do the direct antiguerrilla fighting. They're the ones who are on the ground fighting directly with the Communist Viet Cong.

Q. Are they really the only ones in direct combat?

A. They are the only Americans who are in daily personal combat with the VC, yes.

Q. Are these the new marines?

A. They do a different job from the marines. The marines are shock troops. The Special Forces are not shock troops. They're not assault troops. They are primarily designed to be dropped into, or put into, an area under enemy control and to take native people, train them, and lead them in guerrilla war, or in an antiguerrilla war.

97

The Green Berets instruct a Montagnard tribesman in how to kill his enemies with the latest techniques.

Q. Are the South Vietnamese Special Forces teams of good caliber?

A. Not usually. That's the trouble. Up until recently, the Vietnamese "A" teams have just been soldiers with good political connections. . . .

Q. Are these Americans supposed to be fighting, or are they just training the Vietnamese to fight?

A. They're supposed to be training the Vietnamese to fight, but they're in actual combat themselves. . . .

Q. Do we issue [American weapons] to the Vietnamese too?

A. They did for a while, and the Vietnamese were losing them to the VC.

Q. Are most of the VC weapons captured U.S. weapons?

A. I would say certainly many of them are. For every bunch of weapons you capture from the VC, you find maybe 30 percent were made in the United States. You find a lot of old French weapons—and now you're finding a lot of Chinese copies of Russian weapons. . . .

Q. How many men are going into South Vietnam from the north?

A. It seems to me a never-ending procession.

Q. Is it increasing?

A. It seems to be increasing. We feel it is.

Q. How do they get in there? . . .

A. They almost never come in directly across the border between North and South Vietnam—almost never. They come down over the Laotian border, come in through Tay Ninh province, generally, which it is believed is the headquarters of the whole VC operation.

Q. Is that all in Laos, or in Cambodia too?

A. They come through Laos and Cambodia. I was with several Special Forces camps along the border. The VC come down from North Vietnam and just make a little jog through Laos and into South Vietnam.

Q. How about Communist weapons? Is it true that some are shipped by boat into Cambodia, and then sent across?

A. Not necessarily. Intelligence sources feel that the weapons are coming down from China by junk, coming by sea right to the delta region of the Mekong River, coming directly to the VC in South Vietnam. There just isn't much you can do about it.

Q. Must the U.S. take operational control of Vietnamese Special Forces plus Vietnamese regular forces?

A. Right. Air forces as well as ground forces.

Q. Are you convinced that the U.S. can win this war without going into Laos and into North Vietnam?

A. I'm convinced of that. I'm convinced that it's not necessary to bomb North Vietnam. If you bomb North Vietnam, that isn't going to stop those 80,000 Communists in South Vietnam. No matter what you do to North Vietnam, the guerrillas are still going to be in the south. And they'll get supplied, one way or another. Red China will supply them.

Chapter Six

DIEN BIEN PHU: THE DAY THE WORLD DIDN'T END

> I will say this: there is going to be no involve-
> ment of America in war unless it is a result of
> the constitutional process that is placed upon
> Congress to declare it. Now, let us have that
> clear; and that is the answer.
> —PRESIDENT DWIGHT D. EISENHOWER,
> *March 10, 1953*

THE MOST significant development in the Franco-Vietnamese war
was an event that took place outside the country: the victory of
Mao Tse-tung's Chinese Communists over the Nationalist regime
of Chiang Kai-shek in 1949. For with the advance in 1950 of
Communist armies to the northern Vietnamese borders, Ho Chi
Minh's forces at last had a secure and prolific source of supply.
The French were, of course, fully aware of this danger, and during
1948 and 1949 they had established a chain of border forts along
the Chinese frontier. But in 1950 General Giap, in a series of
surprise attacks, forced their evacuation. This was according to
neither the Maoist nor the French book of warfare. Attacks on
fortified positions (and they were fortified in some strength and
could be supplied by air) were exactly contrary to Mao's doctrine
of guerrilla warfare; the success of such attacks was contrary to
French belief. But Giap was able, through Vietminh political control of the countryside, to secretly assemble large numbers of
troops outside any given fortification. Then, waiting for a rainy or
cloudy day that would hamper effective air support, Vietminh

troops would launch suicidally savage attacks—their leaders aware that they must seize the fortification before air or ground reinforcement could be sent. The French had learned well the guerrilla tactics of the Vietminh—so well that they had become accustomed to them and did not anticipate this sudden change. Fort after fort fell, and Chinese supplies began to roll into the Vietminh camps.

None of which immediately changed the nature of the war. Giap's forces still faced monumental tasks in arming and training men and, as always, gaining political control in ever larger regions of the countryside. Nor were the French without resources. On the political front in Asia they brought into being, out of the old territory of Indochina, two new and independent (within the French Union) states: Laos and Cambodia. By granting these countries their independence and separating them from the "independent" state of Vietnam, the French thought to pacify nationalist aspirations and preclude Laotian and Cambodian support for the Vietminh. And French military activity increased with new vigor as fresh troops and supplies were poured into the struggle and a new and able commander, General Jean de Lattre de Tassigny, was sent out from France. During 1951 De Tassigny's forces were able to clear the Vietminh out of most of the Red River delta area, but De Tassigny's death shortly thereafter jeopardized these temporary gains.

Meanwhile, faced with increased French pressure in Vietnam, the Vietminh extended the war into Laos and Cambodia. After the usual careful political preparation, they set up, in combination with groups of dissatisfied Laotian peasants, an organization (Pathet Lao) to dispute power with the Laotian government. This was the beginning of a prolonged guerrilla war in Laos which both distracted French energies from the struggle in Vietnam and provided the Vietminh with very useful supply trails through the jungles of the long Laos-Vietnam frontier. In Cambodia the Vietminh found natural allies among the dissident Issarak tribesmen of the hills whom they armed and who proved a very effective thorn in the French military flank.

But aside from the tactical military gains won by the Vietminh through spreading the war into Laos and Cambodia, there were deeper political implications. By raising and arming a native Communist opposition in these countries, the Vietminh were demonstrating to the world that Laotian and Cambodian independence within the French Union (or without it, for that matter) was not enough; evidently there were sizable numbers of people in those nations who demanded revolutionary social and economic change as well. And by spreading the war Ho Chi Minh was, in effect, making it more dangerous. The French were now placed in the position of gambling not simply for the domination of Vietnam but for the control of all Southeast Asia—with an increasingly worried and belligerent Red China attentively watching. The possibility of a confrontation between the Chinese and the Americans in this area was thereby increased—to the alarm of thoughtful people throughout the world. It may not be too much to say that the Vietminh penetration of Laos, with all its implications, was the decisive step that was to bring them eventual victory. But in order to understand how this came about, it is necessary to see France's war in Vietnam from an international perspective.

The central fact of life about Asia after 1949 was the emergence of Mao Tse-tung's Chinese People's Republic as the master of the vast Chinese mainland and all its resources and people. His victory over Chiang Kai-shek had been made possible, basically, by several factors. First of all, there was no doubt that the Chinese Communists really understood and supported the aspirations of that country's oppressed and teeming millions, and in turn enjoyed the support of its people. Secondly, Chiang Kai-shek's Nationalist government had, over the years, degenerated into a corrupt, inefficient and increasingly totalitarian regime. Finally, decades of Japanese aggression in China had destroyed much of the fabric of Chinese society. Given these factors, Mao's victory in China would seem to have been all but inevitable, with or without outside assistance. And Mao had received such assistance at the end of World War II when the Russian Army, which had defeated the Japanese in Manchuria, turned over large stocks of weapons and the control of large areas to Mao's forces.

But the "inevitability" of Communist success in China was not acknowledged in the United States. To most Americans, Chiang

Kai-shek symbolized the heroic struggle of the Chinese people against Japan. American sympathies had been with Chiang since 1935, and it was basically Japan's continuing aggression in China and American opposition to it that had made war between Japan and the United States unavoidable in 1941. Thereafter China had been hailed as one of the "Big Four" wartime allies, and the failings of Chiang Kai-shek's regime were discreetly overlooked. During the latter stages of the war, ever larger supplies of American arms found their way to Chiang's forces—despite the fact that the generalissimo refused to use these weapons and the elite American-trained divisions he then possessed against the common enemy, Japan. Instead Chiang was hoarding this new strength for a planned battle to wipe out the Chinese Communists after World War II was won. As victory dawned in the Pacific in August 1945, Chiang's forces were air- and sea-lifted to formerly Japanese-controlled cities and areas all over China by American ships and planes. There was no doubt that this was intended to forestall Communist occupation of these regions. The American commitment to Chiang, supported by the majority of the American people, advocated by a powerful "China Lobby" in Washington composed of politicians representing U.S. commercial interests in China, and backed by a government operating under wartime treaties and agreements, did not end with World War II.

That the United States continued to send arms, advisors and money to Chiang Kai-shek's weak and corrupt government after the war was due basically to a shift in the American perspective toward the Russian-led world Communist movement. The wartime alliance between Stalin's Russia and the western Allies was, by late 1945, clearly headed for trouble. Misunderstandings regarding wartime commitments, disagreements over how postwar Europe should be organized, Russian suspicion of "western capitalist" motives, American alarm over Russia's policy of armed domination of eastern Europe—all these contributed to a growing American conviction that Stalinist Russia was bent on a course of eventual world subversion and conquest. The prospect that China's huge population and vast resources might be added to the Communist camp was unacceptable to the United States. Thus American support for Chiang Kai-shek against Mao Tse-tung began to be seen as a part of a global strategy to "contain" Communist expansion in the postwar world.

And to many Americans this seemed an entirely feasible policy. The United States had, after all, just created in a miraculously short time the mightiest military machine ever seen. Added to that was the fact of American monopoly of atomic weapons. And underneath this military confidence was the old American conviction that whatever the nation set its hand to would be accomplished—it was only a question of effort, loyalty and patriotic confidence in the justice of any American cause.

When, therefore, in spite of all American efforts, Mao Tse-tung's armies (largely supplied with captured American weapons) swept to victory in 1949, both the American people and the American government experienced a rude shock. The fall of Chiang's regime was described in the United States as "the loss of China," as if China had ever been America's to lose. The failure of the American effort there to contain communism was ascribed to inefficiency, subversion and outright treason on the part of American military and government officials. And certain politicians, notably Wisconsin Senator Joseph McCarthy, did not hesitate, for personal political profit, to fan the flames of suspicion and hysteria that swept the nation. It became politically impossible for any American government to both maintain itself in office and adopt a realistic policy toward Red China. Those who calmly pointed out that there were, after all, limits to American power, that short of total war there was not really very much the United States could do to control the desires and destinies of four hundred and fifty million people of an utterly foreign culture and background on the other side of the world—such voices were silenced by accusations of disloyalty.

Yet there was more to American policy in the face of the emergence of Red China than simple hysteria. There was no doubt that Mao Tse-tung's was a totalitarian Communist regime, no matter how much support it enjoyed among China's impoverished masses. Nor was there then any doubt that Mao would ally himself with Stalin's Russia. Furthermore, in the flush of victory, Chinese Communists loudly proclaimed their intentions of helping other countries of Asia to "liberate" themselves from "western colonial oppression." And beyond all of this remained the possibility that when China eventually became fully industrialized, with its immense resources and population, it might one day emerge as one of the world's most powerful nations. If, at that time, China remained Communist, the balance of power between the western democratic-capitalist nations and the Communist world might tip irretrievably against the West. There were, of course, possibilities of influencing Chinese development. China's Communist regime might lose much of its belligerence as it grappled with China's awesome domestic problems; China's policy toward the West might mellow as the memory of colonial exploitation faded and the Chinese increased their contact with the democratic nations; the Chinese-Russian alliance might one day split (with their long common border it seemed possible that China and Russia might find things to quarrel about) as Tito's Yugoslavia had separated itself from Russian-dominated eastern Europe—all of these and other possibilities existed. But to point them out, much less attempt to use American influence to bring them about, was, during the 1950s, politically impossible in the United States. Instead a small but very vocal group of Americans advocated a preventive war against Red China, while the majority accepted a policy of "containing" Red China militarily and shunning her politically in the hope that someday, somehow, the whole problem might simply "go away."

Red Chinese attitudes toward the United States were conditioned basically by Chinese nationalism and by classical Communist views of capitalist democracies. To the Chinese, little distinction could be made between the American intervention in Chinese affairs and the American commercial exploitation of China during the nineteenth century and the more vigorously imperialist practices of such nations as France and England. Chinese nationalism, whether exploited by Communist or by non-Communist leaders, would in any case have driven "western imperialists and colonialists" from China in the not distant future. But since Chinese nationalism was now led by the Chinese Communist Party, it was reinforced by Marxist-Leninist interpretations and predictions regarding the inevitability of bloody clashes between the "decaying" capitalist world and the new socialist states. In particular, American support for Chiang Kai-shek was looked upon as an attempt to maintain a corrupt and "Fascist" government in power so that American commercial interests might continue to exploit China's people and resources. And when, after Chiang and his followers had been driven from the mainland, the United States continued to support them on their island fortress of Formosa, the Chinese regarded this with much the same feelings that northerners after the American Civil War might have had if Jefferson Davis's Confederate government had found refuge in Cuba and had there been protected by Great Britain.

Attitudes and fears on both sides were inflamed when, on June 25, 1950, armies of the Communist Republic of North Korea invaded the territory of South Korea. Korea, long under Japanese domination, had been liberated in the closing days of World War II by Russian forces advancing from the north and American forces landing in the south. It was agreed that both forces would halt at the 38th parallel, primarily to avoid confusion. But when cooperation between the occupation forces in the two zones proved impossible, each proceeded to create a government in its own image in its respective zone. By mid-1949 both Russian and American occupation forces had been withdrawn and the two Korean nations left to face each other belligerently across the 38th parallel. When the North Koreans (not without provocation from the south and encouragement and military support from the Soviet Union) attacked in June 1950, it was assumed that they enjoyed both Russian and Red Chinese backing. An American-led and -equipped United Nations army composed for the most part of American troops was quickly thrown into the struggle. Initial North Korean successes were reversed in September 1950, and UN forces under the command of General Douglas Mac-Arthur swept north to the Korean-Chinese border at the Yalu River. Red China had warned that it would not tolerate so close an advance to its frontier, but these warnings were disregarded. Then, in November 1950, huge Chinese armies (called "volunteers" by Mao Tse-tung's government) intervened and inflicted a disastrous defeat on UN forces. Once again, in the spring of 1951, MacArthur's men advanced, and the battle lines settled down just north of the 38th parallel. Truce talks between the two sides began in July 1951 and continued without much progress for the next two years, while a bloody war of attrition dragged itself out.

At the very opening stages of the Korean War, American President Harry S Truman, fearing that this attack might be the prelude to an all-out Communist offensive throughout Asia, had declared that Chiang Kai-shek's regime on Formosa would henceforth be protected by the United States Seventh Fleet. Any Red Chinese attack on Formosa (or certain other Nationalist controlled offshore islands) would mean war with the United States. At the same time Truman announced that the Chinese Nationalists would not be permitted to attack the Communist mainland—in other words an armed "pax Americana" had been established over all the China Seas.

The Korean War seemed to offer confirmation of the worst American suspicions of Red Chinese intentions in Asia. President Truman's policy of "containment" of the Communist world, begun in Greece at the end of World War II and established in Europe through the creation of the North Atlantic Treaty Organization (NATO), was now definitively extended to Asia. But while NATO was composed of European nations acting together, with American participation, to protect their homelands against potential Russian aggression (American atomic power offering the final deterrent), where could the United States find able and willing allies to aid in "containing" Red China in Asia? Japan was disarmed, occupied and notably disinclined to assume any military burdens after the shattering experience of World War II. India, in the process of throwing off the British yoke, was weak and divided. The islands—the Philippines and Indonesia—could offer little more than bases for American forces (and the Indonesians were engaged in their own war of liberation from Holland). Burma and Malaya (still occupied by Britain) offered some promise—and then of course there was the French presence in Indochina. Unfortunately, the only allies of any value that the United States could find in Asia would be precisely those European colonial powers whose presence there had become hateful to all Asiatics. A NATO structure for the Far East was not a serious possibility to the Truman administration. And further complicating matters was the oft-expressed opinion of American military leaders from General MacArthur all the way back to the Joint Chiefs of Staff in Washington, that the United States must *never* permit itself to become embroiled in a land war on the Asian continent. How then to contain Red Chinese aggression?

The Truman administration remained satisfied to support the UN forces in Korea and establish control over Chinese coastal waters. It was felt that the French in Indochina could handle that flank of the Communist attack, for by 1950 most American government officials had come to see Ho Chi Minh's Vietminh as merely a southern extension of Chinese power as the Republic of North Korea was its northern extension. Accordingly, the United States recognized the new Vietnamese regime of Emperor Bao Dai and the French Union presence in all of Indochina. Moreover, under various agreements, American military, economic and financial aid began to flow into Vietnam—the financial and economic aid directly to Bao Dai's government, the military aid to French forces. In 1950 an American team of military and economic advisors was dispatched to Vietnam to supervise the use of American aid.

When Truman's Democratic Party went down to defeat in the American presidential elections of 1952, it was in no small part due to suspicions and charges generated by the Communist victory in China and the Communist offensives in Korea and Indochina. The new Republican President, Dwight D. Eisenhower, and his Secretary of State, John Foster Dulles, had promised the American electorate both to bring the war in Korea to a satisfactory conclusion and to pursue a more effective policy in containing Communist expansion in Asia. More than that, during the election campaign Dulles had hinted that "containment" was not enough: he looked forward to "rolling back" Communist power throughout the world. As the new administration took up its duties in Washington in 1953 it found itself the inheritor not only of the Korean War but also of the Truman administration's policy of aiding the French and the Bao Dai regime in Indochina.

In line with Eisenhower's promises, a new policy was worked out during 1953. While armistice negotiations were pushed forward in Korea, both the President and Secretary of State Dulles repeatedly warned that no armistice would be concluded in Korea or respected by the United States there if it meant simply that Chinese aggressive power would be shifted to Indochina. In other words, any Chinese massive intervention in Vietnam would re-open the Korean War as well. Furthermore, the American Seventh Fleet was withdrawn from its "quarantine" duties around Formosa—hinting that Chiang Kai-shek might now be "un-leashed" to fulfill his oft-proclaimed promise to reconquer the Chinese mainland. And aid to the French and Bao Dai in Indo-china was stepped up. Over the next three years it would total nearly $1,300,000,000. Americans weapons, ammunition and planes flowed into the Vietnam War—and American technical experts followed them.

The assumptions underlying the new and more aggressive American policy in Asia were threefold. First of all, as Dulles pointed out in an article published in 1950: ". . . there is a civil war in which we have, for better or worse, involved our prestige. Since that is so, we must help the government we have backed. Its defeat . . . would make even more people in the East feel that friendship with the United States is a liability rather than an asset." Secondly, as was stated in the report of a special commis-sion on the Far East headed by Republican Representative Walter Judd: "The area of Indochina is immensely wealthy in rice, rubber, coal and iron ore. Its position makes it a strategic key to the rest of Southeast Asia. If Indochina should fall, Thai-land and Burma would be in extreme danger; Malaya, Singapore, and even Indonesia would become more vulnerable to the Com-munist power drive. . . . The Communists must be prevented from achieving their objectives in Indochina." Thirdly, the Communist drive in Indochina was viewed as part of a worldwide aggression, an expression of a monolithic centrally directed operation headed by the rulers of the Soviet Union. Any capitulation in Indochina would simply embolden the Russians to undertake further aggres-sions elsewhere, perhaps in Europe itself.

Thus early were established the arguments that have been ad-vanced ever since for ever-increasing American participation in Vietnam: that American prestige would suffer an irreversible blow if Vietnam fell, thereby divesting the United States of its allies throughout the world; that, like dominoes on end, if Vietnam fell to the Communists, one by one the other states of Southeast Asia would tumble over into the Communist camp; and that any capitulation to the Vietminh in Vietnam would be "appeasement," that Russia and China, like Hitler's Germany before World War II, would look upon any American withdrawal from Vietnam as a sign of weakness that would only embolden them to push more aggressively elsewhere and would eventually lead to World War III. Later we will consider the validity of these theories in greater detail. For the moment we must see what effect they had on the continuing war between France and the Vietminh.

All during 1951 and 1952, Red Chinese aid to the Vietminh increased. Vietminh forces were trained in China and advised by Chinese military experts during operations against the French. More and more heavy weapons were supplied to Ho's men. General Giap was now dealing, not with guerrilla bands, but with regular Vietminh Army forces organized in battalion and even divisional strength. Clearly the Vietminh, with Chinese backing, were preparing for a decisive drive against the French, during which they would even be willing to risk open, regular warfare. To test his new organization and to keep the French off balance, Giap invaded Laos with over 40,000 men in April 1953 and nearly captured the Laotian capital of Luang Prabang before withdrawing as the heavy rains of the monsoon season set in. Though the French and Laotian Royal Army forces were able to reclaim much of the area won by the Vietminh, it was very evident that the war in Indochina was entering a new phase.

This new phase was not entirely unwelcome to the French military and to the French government. France, eager to escape some of the burdens of its endless war in Indochina, had welcomed American participation—and had never ceased to point out that its loss of Vietnam would mean a decisive *American* defeat in Asia also, though no Americans were engaged in combat there. The prospect of an "open," regular offensive by Vietminh forces was eagerly awaited by French officers. This would give them a chance to use their superior firepower, air power and military organization; it would convert the losing guerrilla war into something with which they were prepared to cope. Giap's soldiers would throw themselves on the French and be destroyed in the process.

The French commander in Indochina, General Henri Navarre, decided to prepare a trap. The Vietminh invasion of Laos had alarmed the French, and to prevent another such invasion Navarre decided to establish a very strong fortified zone in and around the village of Dien Bien Phu, from which area the French could stop any Vietminh drive into Laos. Furthermore, such a strong point would surely lure General Giap's men into a massive attack against it—and such an attack, which would certainly fail in the face of superior French firepower and resources, might well break the back of the Vietminh Army. Dien Bien Phu was to be a French "Gibraltar" in the hilly jungle border area between Laos and Vietnam, a Gibraltar that could be endlessly supplied and reinforced by air, and one against which the Vietminh would dash itself to pieces. Accordingly, in the fall of 1953, French forces established their "impregnable" position at Dien Bien Phu and awaited the outcome. Giap obliged, and in mid-January 1954 he attacked the "strong point."

But General Navarre made several serious miscalculations. For one thing, he had chosen an area that could be dominated from the surrounding hills. For another, Dien Bien Phu was at the extreme range possible to the French fighter planes based in Laos and Vietnam that were expected to support the base. He also miscalculated the amount of artillery available to the Vietminh and how they would use it. Red China had supplied Giap's forces with far more heavy artillery than was generally supposed by the French. And instead of employing it in the classical manner—that is, hiding it behind the hills around Dien Bien Phu to protect it from the French artillery, thereby placing it out of range of the most important French forts—the Vietminh, under cover of night, dug their artillery right into the forward slopes of the hills and camouflaged it heavily. Thus they were able to fire at the French forts point-blank and with devastating effect. Using this tactic the Vietminh were soon able to knock out most of the French artillery and thus were able to creep closer to the French forts and launch massive ground attacks. Furthermore, with the

French artillery knocked out, the Vietminh were able to bring their own antiaircraft guns so close to the French perimeter that furnishing supplies to Dien Bien Phu by air became all but impossible. After a few months only parachute drops were possible, and these only from such high altitudes that many French supplies missed the restricted target and fell into Vietminh hands.

Another serious mistake in French planning was the assumption that Giap and his men, used to primitive guerrilla tactics, would never be able to undertake regular siege operations. But this was precisely what Giap did. Over the months of combat he pushed forward a complex series of trenches around the beleaguered forts in the manner of a true, classical siege. By the middle of March 1954 the French at Dien Bien Phu were in deep difficulties. It was apparent that unless something was done, and quickly, the Vietminh would win an overwhelming victory.

This impending Vietminh victory would have implications more far-reaching than anyone had foreseen, because the United States, Britain, France, Russia and Red China had already agreed to hold a conference in Geneva, Switzerland, to be opened on April 26, 1954, to discuss the Indochina problem and find a solution to it as well as other Far Eastern matters. If Red China and the Vietminh came to such a conference after a smashing victory over the French at Dien Bien Phu, they would be in a much better bargaining position to press forward Vietminh claims. Furthermore, Red Chinese confidence, emboldened by a victory over the French, might well jeopardize the negotiations just then getting under way again to bring the Korean War to a final end. The United States had accepted French confidence in the Navarre plan—but now it seemed that disaster loomed.

On March 20, 1954, General Paul Ely, French chief of staff, hurried to Washington. There he informed the American Joint Chiefs of Staff, headed by Admiral Arthur W. Radford, that the French position at Dien Bien Phu remained secure—but he wanted the promise of American intervention if Red China intervened by air. He found, however, that American information (proceeding from U.S. military advisors in Vietnam) was different from the French. The American military were seriously worried about Dien Bien Phu. They proposed to General Ely that the United States Air Force, based in the Philippines, launch a massive night raid against Vietminh positions around Dien Bien Phu. This plan, labeled Operation Vulture, called for the use of about 60 B-29 heavy bombers, escorted by more than 150 fighters from the Seventh Fleet—and if the first raid did not wipe out Vietminh siege positions, further raids were proposed. General Ely promised to present these plans to his government in Paris for consideration.

The French hesitation over accepting direct American air intervention at Dien Bien Phu was based on the fact that France had reached the end of the line in Indochina. The French people demanded peace there, and the French government was counting on the forthcoming Geneva Conference to enable it to get out of the Vietnamese quagmire. An American air strike might provoke Chinese retaliation—and, worse than that, it might upset the Geneva meeting. It was evident to the French that while they hoped primarily to get out of Vietnam salvaging as much as possible, the Americans were primarily interested in maintaining a strong military presence there as part of a regional power base in Southeast Asia from which to confront Red China.

By April 3, the situation at Dien Bien Phu had degenerated so alarmingly that the Americans thought the time had come to act. But to undertake massive intervention in Vietnam, even purely through air power, would require congressional support. Accordingly, Secretary of State Dulles and President Eisenhower assembled a representative body of congressional leaders at the State Department to secure such support. Admiral Radford informed the senators and representatives that Dien Bien Phu would certainly fall unless the United States intervened. He outlined the proposed Operation Vulture. There was a moment of painful silence before the congressmen shot back their questions.

Would not this American air strike be an act of outright war?

Secretary Dulles admitted it would.

Would not the Chinese intervene?

Secretary Dulles was not certain but believed the Chinese would back down before such a show of force.

Did the United States enjoy the support of its allies in conducting this operation?

Secretary Dulles admitted that no other nations had been consulted.

Would American land forces be necessary if the air strike failed?

Admiral Radford could not be certain.

Did Admiral Radford enjoy the support of the other Joint Chiefs of Staff for this plan?

Admiral Radford declared that the others were all opposed to it; only he favored it.

The congressmen were obviously alarmed—and very unwilling to support the administration's plan: certainly not unless the United States could enlist the full cooperation of its allies.

But during the next few days Secretary of State Dulles learned that the French were opposed to the American plan because they feared it would undermine the Geneva Conference—and still remained skeptical as to its necessity. On the other hand, British Prime Minister Sir Winston Churchill was adamantly opposed to the American plan because he foresaw that it might well be the first step on the road to World War III. When, later in April, the French finally realized that their garrison at Dien Bien Phu was doomed, they panicked and suddenly asked the United States to undertake Operation Vulture after all—and quickly. But Britain remained firmly opposed, and American public opinion as reflected in congressional attitudes was not encouraging. Operation Vulture was shelved.

Meanwhile, General Giap's men were inching ever closer to the forts at Dien Bien Phu. Under the rain of Vietminh artillery fire, life within the restricted French camp became a veritable hell. Supplies of ammunition, food and medicines ran lower and lower. There came a point when air drops could no longer be made. The case of the wounded was pitiful: they could not be evacuated, nor could they be properly treated in the beleaguered camp. One by one the French forts fell to massive attacks by Vietminh infantrymen. At last, on May 7, 1954, General Giap's forces entered the central French stronghold at Dien Bien Phu, which now surrendered. The Vietminh took more than ten thousand prisoners there—and their victory symbolized the destruction of French power throughout Indochina. After seven years of struggle, Ho Chi Minh's forces, fighting "the war of the flea," had indeed ripped the guts out of the French elephant.

A Chat with Chairman Mao

EARLY IN 1965 Edgar Snow, American author and expert on Far Eastern affairs, was granted an interview with Mao Tse-tung in Peking. Mr. Snow was permitted to publish Chairman Mao's comments—but without direct quotation. Some excerpts:

"Can Viet-Cong forces now win victory by their own efforts?"

Yes, he [Chairman Mao] thought they could. Their position was relatively better than that of the Communists during the first civil war (1927–37) in China. At that time there was no direct foreign intervention, but now already the Viet Cong had the American intervention to help arm and educate the rank and file and the army officers. Those opposed to the United States were no longer confined to the liberation army. . . . The American teachers were succeeding.

In reply to a specific question, the chairman affirmed that there were no Chinese forces in northern Vietnam or anywhere else in Southeast Asia. China had no troops outside her own frontiers.

"Dean Rusk has often stated that if China would give up her aggressive policies, the United States would withdraw from Vietnam. What does he mean?"

Chairman Mao Tse-tung in 1967.

Mao replied that China had no policies of aggression to abandon. China had committed no acts of aggression. China gave
support to revolutionary movements but not by sending troops.
Of course, whenever a liberation struggle existed China would
publish statements and call demonstrations to support it. It was
precisely that which vexed the imperialists. . . .

Some Americans had said that the Chinese revolution was led
by Russian aggressors, but in truth the Chinese revolution was
armed by Americans. In the same way the Vietnamese revolution
was also being armed by Americans, not by China. The liberation
forces had not only greatly improved their supplies of American
weapons during recent months but also expanded their forces by
recruiting American-trained troops and officers from the puppet
armies of South Vietnam. China's liberation forces had grown in
numbers and strength by recruiting to their side the troops
trained and armed by the Americans for Chiang Kai-shek. The

movement was called "changing of hats." When Nationalist soldiers changed hats in large numbers because they knew the peasants would kill them for wearing the wrong hat, then the end was near. "Changing hats" was becoming more popular now among the Vietnamese puppets.

Mao said that the conditions for revolutionary victory in China had been, first, that the ruling group was weak and incompetent, led by a man who was always losing battles. Second, the People's Liberation Army was strong and able, and people believed in its cause. In places where such conditions did not prevail the Americans could intervene. Otherwise, they would stay away or soon leave.

"Do you mean that the circumstances of victory for the Liberation Front now exist in South Vietnam?"

Mao thought that the American forces were not yet ready to leave. Fighting would go on perhaps for one or two years. After that the United States troops would find it boring and might go home or somewhere else.

"Under existing circumstances," he was asked, "do you really see any hope of an improvement in Sino-American relations?"

Yes, he thought there was hope. It would take time. Maybe there would be no improvement in his generation. He was soon going to see God. According to the laws of dialectics all contradictions must finally be resolved, including the struggle of the individual.

Chapter Seven

GENEVA: COLLAPSE AND RESPONSE

> I am convinced that American military aid, no
> matter how extensive, cannot crush an enemy
> who is everywhere and nowhere . . . an enemy of
> the people who at the same time commands the
> support and sympathy of the entire people . . .
> —SENATOR JOHN F. KENNEDY, 1954

THE CONFERENCE of Foreign Ministers to discuss Asian affairs
opened at Geneva on April 27, 1954. On May 8, just as word came
of the fall of Dien Bien Phu, the conferees, who had been fruit-
lessly wrangling over Korean matters, turned to the situation in
Indochina. French Foreign Minister Georges Bidault, his voice
choked with tears, began the discussion with a eulogy to his
nation's fallen soldiers. Britain's foreign secretary, Anthony Eden;
Red China's commissar for foreign affairs, Chou En-lai; Russia's
foreign minister, Vyacheslav Molotov; and American "diplomatic observer" Walter Bedell Smith (Secretary of State John
Foster Dulles had left Geneva on May 4, clearly not wishing to be
associated with any possible "concessions" to communism)
listened respectfully. Everyone present knew that France had
irrevocably lost the war in Indochina; Dien Bien Phu, however
stunning a defeat, only symbolized the fact that the Vietminh
now controlled at least two-thirds of all Vietnam—and could expect support from armed Communist groups in Laos and Cambodia as well.

The foreign ministers of the "Great Powers" were not the only participants at Geneva. Also present at the conference table were representatives from the Vietminh and from the French-sponsored Vietnam government of Bao Dai. Bao Dai, as chief of state, had appointed the ardently nationalist and Catholic politician Ngo Dinh Diem to be premier of the Vietnamese government; Diem in turn had sent Vietnamese foreign minister Dr. Tran Van Do to Geneva.

Dr. Tran Van Do, a man of unquestioned integrity and fierce patriotism, represented a government which, however shaky its authority, had at French insistence summoned nearly 280,000 Vietnamese to serve in the Vietnamese Army that collaborated with the 200,000-man French expeditionary force against Ho Chi Minh's followers. Diem's government had succeeded in bringing Vietminh-inspired acts of terrorism to a halt in Saigon, and even in clearing certain areas of the Mekong River delta of Vietminh guerrillas. But Dr. Tran soon learned that the views of the French puppet government at Saigon were of no consequence, even to the French.

The Vietminh, called now the Democratic Republic of Vietnam, were represented by Pham Van Dong—next only to General Giap, perhaps Ho Chi Minh's trustiest lieutenant. And despite Vietminh victories, Pham Van Dong clearly went to Geneva with instructions to compromise, not attempt to dictate, during negotiations. In fact the Vietminh accepted at Geneva considerably less than their successful seven-year-struggle might seem to have warranted. Ho Chi Minh himself, in an address to the members of the Vietminh Central Committee, explained this policy of moderation:

"The following errors might occur: leftist deviationism—people intoxicated by our continual victories will want to fight at any price, fight to the end. Like men who cannot see the woods for the trees, they are mindful of the enemy's withdrawal yet pay no heed to his maneuverings; they see the French but not the Americans; they are full of enthusiasm for military action and underestimate diplomatic action. They do not understand that side by side with armed battle we are carrying on our campaign at the international conferences, with the same objective in view.

. . . They put forward excessive conditions, unacceptable to the other side. They want to rush everything, and do not realize that the struggle for peace is hard and complex. . . ." Ho Chi Minh had been fighting patiently all his life; a little more patience was not impossible to him. When General Giap had brought him the news of the great Vietminh victory at Dien Bien Phu, Ho had replied gently: "However great the victory, it is only a beginning."

At first both the Vietminh and the Diem government pressed the conference to hold nationwide elections throughout Vietnam to be supervised by an international authority, possibly the United Nations. But the western nations clearly saw that such elections would result in an overwhelming victory for Ho Chi Minh. As President Eisenhower stated later: "I have never talked or corresponded with a person knowledgeable in Indochinese affairs who did not agree that had elections been held as of the time of the fighting, possibly 80 percent of the population would have voted for the Communist Ho Chi Minh as their leader rather than Chief of State Bao Dai." Dr. Tran Van Do was advised to forgo elections. It is not entirely clear why the Vietminh representative, Pham Van Dong, did not insist upon immediate elections, conscious as he must have been of their inevitable result. It is thought that Red China's foreign minister, Chou En-lai, anxious to reach a general settlement with the West that would encompass other Asiatic problems, successfully pressured the Vietminh delegation into postponing elections. In any event, with agreement on this thorny issue the conference settled into a round of bargaining over just how much territory should be left under the Vietminh and how much under Diem's authority. The French were, in any case, to withdraw from all of Indochina.

The Final Declaration by the conference contained the following major provisions:

1. Both Vietminh and Franco-Vietnamese forces were to be withdrawn so that the Vietminh controlled Vietnamese territory north of the 17th parallel, while Diem's forces controlled the area south of this line. A demilitarized zone just on the 17th parallel was to be established to separate the combatants.

2. *All* foreign troops were to be withdrawn from all of Indo-

While the diplomats argued in Geneva, the people of Hanoi waited ...

The French presence in Saigon would soon be but a memory and a lingering cultural influence.

china, and no foreign nations were to provide arms or military aid to either side. Neither was any foreign power to establish any military base anywhere in Indochina.

3. Neither North nor South Vietnam would undertake reprisals against people sympathetic with the opposite side within their territories. Those who wished to move from one zone to the other would freely be permitted to do so.

4. Neither side was to intervene, directly or indirectly, in the internal affairs of the other in any manner whatsoever. Nor was either side to establish any kind of economic blockade against the other: there was to be free passage of goods between them.

5. Neither side was to adhere to any military alliance, either western or Communist.

6. The military withdrawals and partitioning of the country along the 17th parallel were to be recognized as temporary. General, nationwide elections that would bring about unification of the entire country were to be held not later than July 1956 under international supervision.

7. An International Commission for Supervision and Control (ICSC), composed of Canadian, Polish and Indian representatives, was to supervise the cease-fire provisions.

One of the remarkable things about this Geneva Declaration was that it was an *unsigned* document. Only the particular military technicalities agreed upon between the Vietminh and French high commands respecting troop withdrawals were signed by the two principals involved as formal agreements. The Declaration itself was in the nature of a communique. When in later years either side violated any part of the Declaration, it could claim that it had never, after all, signed any agreement.

Another remarkable feature of the Geneva Declaration was that the United States, one of the parties heavily involved in the Indochina war (to the tune of more than one billion dollars), refused to associate itself with the Declaration in any way whatsoever. It will be recalled that the Eisenhower administration, sensitive to charges of "being soft on communism" (it had come to power using that charge against the Democrats), had already downgraded its mission to Geneva to the status of "observers." Now,

Walter Bedell Smith, chief American "observer," declared that "my government is not prepared to join in a declaration by the conference such as is submitted." Instead he read out a separate American declaration that included a promise by the United States to "refrain from the threat or the use of force to disturb" the agreements.

The Geneva Declaration was issued on July 20, 1954. On October 10 Ho Chi Minh returned once again to Hanoi—after eight years of incessant guerrilla struggle. But with so much of the nation in ruins, few felt like celebrating. Cheering was reserved for the victory parade of General Giap's veteran troops; the government of the Democratic Republic of Vietnam resumed its duties in Hanoi with little pomp and less ceremony.

There was much to do. Almost 190,000 French and Vietnamese troops had to be evacuated to the area south of the 17th parallel. About 80,000 Vietminh guerrillas and sympathizers went north, while 860,000 northerners (mostly Catholics) trudged south. About 5,000 Vietminh hard-core guerrilla leaders remained in the south but went underground. They hid their weapons and communications equipment and became anonymous villagers. In Saigon and Hué, Vietminh adherents formed legal political organizations to promote the slogan "Peace and Reunification in Two Years." Such organizations were quickly disbanded by the Diem government's police, however, and many of their leaders arrested.

The government of what was rapidly coming to be known as "South Vietnam" (although according to the Geneva Declaration there was but one Vietnam, divided into two *temporary* military occupation zones), headed by Chief of State Bao Dai and run by Premier Ngo Dinh Diem, had seen its interests largely ignored at Geneva. Its representative there, Dr. Tran Van Do, had cabled Diem: "Absolutely impossible to surmount the hostility of our enemies and the perfidy of false friends. . . ." And indeed, the Geneva Declaration placed the Diem government in a difficult position. After all, the great majority of Vietnamese, north and south, had supported the struggle for independence for decades— and Ho Chi Minh had been the symbol of that struggle to southern no less than northern Vietnamese. Any government ruling in

Saigon, in order to win popular support, would itself have to be highly nationalistic—and would somehow have to convince its people that *its* brand of nationalism was preferable to Ho Chi Minh's brand—the only brand so many Vietnamese had ever really been familiar with. Yet the Bao Dai–Diem regime needed, for the moment at least, the continued presence and support of French troops. North Vietnam had a population of more than fifteen million and included almost all the nation's industry; South Vietnam held a population of less than twelve million and was primarily agricultural. If the Diem government was to survive it would have to find ways and means of escaping the Geneva Declaration, for elections held in two years would produce the same result as elections held immediately: an overwhelming victory for Ho Chi Minh.

Thus, from the very beginning, the government of South Vietnam denounced the Geneva accords, signed, as they held, by a foreign military command (the French) "in contempt of Vietnamese national interests." Diem's government refused to discuss the coming elections with North Vietnamese representatives, refused to open normal postal communications between the northern and southern zones, and refused to enter into any economic agreements with the north. This last was a serious blow to Ho Chi Minh's government in Hanoi, for the north depended on the importation of southern rice to make up its food deficit; until then the northern province had received an average of 200,000 tons of rice each year from the south. This amounted to an economic blockade of the north by the south—something expressly forbidden by the Geneva Declaration. Diem declared: "We cannot entertain any Communist proposal as long as we do not have evidence that they place the interests of the Fatherland above those of communism."

Diem, intent on winning for himself and his government the role of true nationalists and anticolonialists before his own people, rapidly divested himself of the signs, symbols and embarrassments of the continuing French presence in the south. First, in 1955 he arranged a plebiscite (an internal election) to decide whether Bao Dai should continue as head of state. The old ex-emperor's image was certainly tarnished through his association with both the French and the Japanese imperialists, and his style of life had little to recommend it to the Vietnamese masses. Yet it is certain that Diem "rigged" the election, for Bao Dai was overthrown and Diem chosen new head of state by 98.8 percent of the voters —a plurality of which even Joseph Stalin might have been proud when he stood for "election" from his own Moscow district. Thereafter Bao Dai exiled himself to the French Riviera, where he lived the luxurious life to which he had always been accustomed. A year later, in February 1956, Diem felt secure enough to demand the withdrawal of the last French troops left in Saigon. France, then embroiled in yet another losing colonial war (in Algeria), was only too happy to comply. On April 26, 1956, the French High Command in Indochina was dissolved—and France had finally extricated itself absolutely from the Indochina quagmire.

And what of the International Commission for Supervision and Control established at Geneva? Its Canadian, Polish and Indian members found themselves all but completely frustrated in accomplishing their duties. Commission members were not allowed to move about freely in North Vietnam and were treated with hostility in the south. Diem-organized mobs attacked ICSC headquarters in Saigon on the first anniversary of the Geneva agreement; in the north, ICSC members were constantly accused of espionage. The ICSC reported in 1956 that North Vietnam, in violation of the Geneva accords, had increased its armed forces from seven to twenty divisions—and these were being armed by Russia and China. On the other hand, it also reported that the Diem regime in South Vietnam, again contrary to the Geneva agreements, was persecuting large numbers of former Vietminh adherents (Diem had established concentration camps to deal with them), was receiving substantial military assistance from the United States, and by permitting the continued presence of an American military mission had, in fact if not in name, entered into an alliance with one of the world power blocs. In its report of January 1957 the commission stated: "While the commission has experienced difficulties in North Viet-Nam, the major part of its difficulties has arisen in South Viet-Nam."

This should not have been surprising. Diem had always felt

that the Geneva Declaration, and all its provisions, had been forced upon him by the French. He therefore had little enthusiasm for the ICSC. On the other hand Ho Chi Minh, confident that the coming elections in July 1956 would certainly establish his government's authority over all of Vietnam, had little to lose by cooperating with the ICSC. Indeed, from 1954 to 1956 the government of North Vietnam scrupulously refrained from any sort of interference in the affairs of the south and, with the exception of those parts dealing with the expansion of armed forces, kept fairly closely to both the letter and the spirit of the Geneva Declaration. Why, after all, should Ho risk international disapproval when he had only to wait peacefully for the elections to give him victory?

But would there be elections? As the date, July 20, 1956, approached, there were ominous signs that they might not take place. The Diem government constantly denounced the Geneva Declaration and took pains to point to North Vietnamese noncompliance in the matter of increases in the North Vietnamese Army. A very clear indication of where the United States stood in the matter was given by Assistant Secretary of State Walter S. Robertson on June 1, 1956, when he declared that North Vietnam had already violated the Geneva agreements—again because of the North Vietnamese Army buildup.

It might be well to pause here to examine the rights and wrongs of those accusations and the importance that ought to have been attached to them. First of all, it was certainly true that the North Vietnamese Army had been dramatically increased in size, and it had received very large amounts of equipment from China and Russia. All of this was contrary to the Geneva agreements. On the other hand, the South Vietnamese Army had also been increased in size and was receiving equipment and advice from the United States. Thus both sides had violated the Geneva Declaration on this point—and for much the same reason; neither Diem nor Ho felt that the foreign powers at Geneva had any right to dictate the *domestic* policies of the respective governments, and the size of a nation's armed forces is certainly a domestic matter. Only if these forces were used outside the national territory would their composition or even existence be of international concern.

And since elections in Vietnam were to be held *before* the two zones were united (indeed, as a precondition to their reunification) and under international supervision, it is hard to see what real objection either side could have made to the increases both undertook in their military power. There was never any suggestion that either the northern or southern Vietnamese armies would be used (or could be used, under international supervision) to influence the coming elections.

Yet these accusations provided the excuse used by Diem, with American backing, to refuse to hold the July 20, 1956, elections promised at Geneva. As that date passed (largely without overt incidents) it became apparent that there would be no elections in Vietnam; that the division of the nation between northern and southern governments was to be permanent. The real reasons behind this are very obvious. Both Diem and his American backers knew very well that Ho Chi Minh would win any such election easily. This would be the end of the Diem government—and it would be the end of the American presence in South Vietnam. If Diem had no desire to divest himself of power, the Americans had no desire to see all of Vietnam under Ho's rule. To them, that meant automatically that Vietnam would become a Chinese-dominated Communist bastion, a power base for continuing Chinese expansion into Southeast Asia—and it was the Chinese-American confrontation in Asia with which American policy makers remained primarily concerned. A South Vietnam that remained independent, on the other hand, could provide a powerful American base from which to "contain" Chinese influence and expansion in the Far East. Furthermore, 1956 was an American election year. It would never do for the Eisenhower administration to permit Vietnam to "go Communist" a few months before election day—that would provide exactly the same kind of political ammunition to the Democrats that the Republicans had used against them in 1952 over Korea.

That American concern over Vietnam had more to do with American fears of Red China than with the rights or wrongs or the nature of the controversy between north and south regarding the Geneva Declaration was made apparent earlier with the establishment of the Southeast Asia Treaty Organization (SEATO) in September 1954. Secretary of State John Foster Dulles, with the humiliating collapse of such American initiatives as Operation Vulture still fresh in his memory, lost no time in seeking to find formal allies for American policy in Asia. Congressional leaders, it will be recalled, had refused support for Operation Vulture on the grounds that the United States could enlist no Allied support for that project. During the next few months Secretary Dulles devoted himself to remedying that situation should another crisis ever develop in the Far East. The SEATO treaty was signed by the governments of Australia, France, New Zealand, Pakistan, the Philippines, Thailand, Great Britain and the United States. Although none of the nations of Indochina were parties to the SEATO agreement, South Vietnam, Laos and Cambodia were added, by special protocol, to the area covered by the treaty's defense and economic provisions. The SEATO countries pledged themselves to regard any "aggression by armed attack" upon any one of them as an aggression committed upon all. In other words, should Red China, for example, attack Thailand or New Zealand, all the members of SEATO, including the United States, would be compelled to go directly to its aid in all-out military support. But it was recognized by the SEATO countries that aggression might not take the form of "armed attack." It might well take the form of subversion instead. In that case the SEATO nations were committed only to "consult immediately in order to agree on the measures which should be taken for the common defense." There was, therefore, no *obligation* under the SEATO treaty for the United States to undertake to support any government threatened by domestic civil war, either militarily or in any other way.

The distinction noted above was underlined by Secretary of State Dulles himself in a speech made in June 1954, a few months before the SEATO pact was signed. Dulles stated: "The situation in Indochina is not that of open military aggression by the Chinese Communist regime. Thus, in Indochina, the problem is one of restoring tranquility in an area where disturbances are fomented from Communist China, but where there is no open invasion from Communist China." As to what measures should be used to deal with that situation, Secretary Dulles was very clear, at least, about what would *not* work: "This task of pacification, in our opinion, cannot be successfully met merely by unilateral armed intervention."

What were the conditions under which the United States might find itself obliged to intervene militarily in Indochina? Dulles declared: "These conditions were and are (1) an invitation from the present lawful authorities; (2) clear assurance of complete independence to Laos, Cambodia and Vietnam; (3) evidence of concern by the United Nations; (4) a joining in the collective effort by some of the other nations in the area; and (5) assurance that France will not itself withdraw from the battle until it is won. Only if these conditions were realized could the President and the Congress be justified in asking the American people to make the sacrifices incident to committing our Nation, with others, to using force to help restore peace in the area."

Direct American relations with the Diem government in South Vietnam were the subject of a letter sent by President Eisenhower to Diem on October 23, 1954. In this letter Eisenhower declared he was instructing the American ambassador in Saigon to enter into discussions with Diem as to "how an intelligent program of American aid given directly to your government can serve to assist Viet-Nam in its present hour of trial, provided that your Government is prepared to give assurances as to the standards of performance it would be able to maintain in the event such aid were supplied.

"The Government of the United States," Eisenhower went on, "expects that this aid will be met by performance on the part of the Government of Viet-Nam in undertaking needed reforms."

President Eisenhower's letter promised only that the United States would "examine" ways and means of providing support for Diem's government—and then only on condition that the Diem regime undertake a program of "reforms" within its own territory.

If we have examined both the SEATO agreements and President Eisenhower's letter to President Diem it is because these are the basic documents to which subsequent American administrations would refer when they spoke of America's "pledge," "commitment," or "word of honor" to defend the South Vietnamese government. Yet under the SEATO pact (to which, it must be remembered, Vietnam was never a party) the United States never committed itself to fighting a war in Indochina except in the case of open armed aggression by some foreign power (and even in that case, the United States was committed to defending the territory of *member nations* of the SEATO treaty, not those who never signed it).

And, in a broader view, Secretary of State Dulles's speech in which he listed the conditions under which the United States might find itself compelled to fight in Indochina was precisely *not* a pledge to do so *unless those conditions were met*. Over the years, as we shall see, only the first of Dulles's conditions was to be met—and even that one, under the circumstances, would be questionable.

In other words, the Eisenhower administration never did "pledge" or "commit" the United States to intervene in Vietnam. It quite wisely left itself a choice of alternatives—and bequeathed that choice to successive American administrations. It did promise to explore ways and means of strengthening the South Vietnamese nation domestically through financial and economic aid, *provided* that the South Vietnamese government itself undertook to make "needed reforms" at home.

Nor is it necessary to quibble over the "letter" of either the SEATO pact or the statements of Dulles and Eisenhower. American intentions and the "spirit" behind them were very well demonstrated by the fact that over the next few years United States aid to South Vietnam was to be three-quarters economic and only one-quarter military. Furthermore, this military aid took the form only of the shipment of equipment and munitions; as late as May 5, 1960, the American Military Assistance and Advisory Group in South Vietnam would number no more that 327 men.

As to whether the South Vietnamese government undertook to make those much-needed reforms on which even this kind of American aid was supposedly based—to examine that we must take a very close look at the developing new state of South Vietnam.

CLOSE-UP

Interrogation

IN ANY WAR the eliciting of information from captured enemy prisoners is a standard procedure. According to international convention, prisoners of war are required to disclose to their captors only their names, ranks and serial numbers. Of course in wartime intelligence officers of all armies adopt various and sometimes highly ingenious means to frighten, trick or fool prisoners into revealing more. Although contrary to various international agreements, such "mental torture" has generally been tacitly accepted as within the admittedly brutal bounds of behavior that inflame all combatants during a war. Physical torture and the murder of prisoners of war have never been acceptable and were crimes imputed to both German and Japanese military men during World War II, for which many of them were subsequently executed. Examples of certain interrogations of Viet Cong and North Vietnamese prisoners of war by both American and South Vietnamese military men, as reported by American journalists and observers, follow:

"One of the most infamous methods of torture used by the government [South Vietnamese] forces is partial electrocution— or 'frying,' as one U.S. advisor calls it. This correspondent was present on the occasion when the torture was employed. Two wires were attached to the thumbs of a Viet Cong prisoner. At the other end of the strings was a field generator, cranked by a Vietnamese private. The mechanism produced an electrical current that burned and shocked the prisoner."

(New York *Herald Tribune*, April 25, 1965)

"Other techniques usually designed to force onlooking prisoners to talk involve cutting off fingers, ears, fingernails or sexual organs of another prisoner. Sometimes a string of ears decorates the wall of a government military installation. One American installation has a Viet Cong ear preserved in alcohol."

(New York *Herald Tribune*, April 25, 1965)

U.S. marines demanding more than "name, rank and serial number" from a captured Viet Cong soldier.

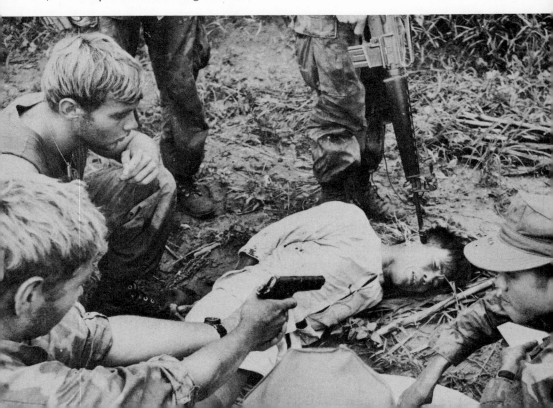

"Many a news correspondent has seen the hands whacked off prisoners with machetes. Prisoners are sometimes castrated or blinded. In more than one case a Viet Cong suspect has been towed after interrogation behind an armored personnel carrier across the rice fields. This always results in death in one of its most painful forms. Vietnamese troops also take their share of enemy heads. . . ."

(*The New Face of War* by Malcolm Browne)

"A helicopter pilot looked up from his Jack Daniel's-and-Coke to relate what had happened to a captive he had been flying back from a battle area. A Vietnamese army officer yelled in the ear of the suspected guerrilla who was tied hand and foot. The man did not respond, so the officer and a Vietnamese soldier heaved him, struggling against his ropes, out of the UH-1B helicopter from 2,900 feet. Then over the roar of the engine, the officer began to interrogate another prisoner who watched wide-eyed. The answers must have been satisfactory, the flier said, because, though kicked and roughly handled, the guerrilla was alive to be marched off when the helicopter landed."

(*The Nation*, December 21, 1964)

"Two Viet Cong prisoners were interrogated on an airplane flying toward Saigon. The first refused to answer questions and was thrown out of the airplane at 3,000 feet. The second immediately answered all the questions. But he too was thrown out."

(New York *Herald Tribune*, April 25, 1965)

". . . several villagers were rounded up and one man was brought before the company commander. The Vietnamese officer briefly questioned the suspect, then turned to his [American] advisor . . . and said, 'I think I shoot this man. Okay?'

" 'Go ahead,' said the advisor.

"The officer fired a carbine round point-blank, striking the villager below the chest. The man slumped and died. The patrol moved on. Later, a correspondent asked the advisor, who had seemed a decent enough fellow, why he had given his approval.

". . . 'These people could have moved to a Government area. In this war they are either on our side or they are not. There is no in-between.' "

(*New York Times Magazine*, November 28, 1965)

"The enemy were very cocky and started shouting anti-American slogans and Vietnamese curses at their captors. The Marines . . . simply lined up the seventeen guerrillas and shot them down in cold blood. . . ."

(*The Making of a Quagmire* by David Halberstam)

"In one place nearby the Americans found three North Vietnamese wounded. One lay huddled under a tree, a smile on his face. 'You won't smile any more,' said one of the American soldiers, pumping bullets into his body. The other two met the same fate."

(*Reuters News Service*, November 16, 1965)

"After surrounding the village . . . the Marines poured in 3.5-inch rocket fire, M-79 grenade launchers and heavy and light machine-gun fire. The Marines then moved in, proceeding first with cigarette lighters, then with flame throwers, to burn down an estimated 150 dwellings. . . . The day's operation netted about four prisoners—old men."

(CBS Television News, August 4, 1965)

Chapter Eight

THE RISE AND FALL OF "DIEMOCRACY"

> If you want war, nourish a doctrine. Doctrines
> are the most frightful tyrants to which men are
> ever subject, because doctrines get inside of a
> man's reason and betray him against himself.
> Civilized men have done their fiercest fighting
> for doctrines.
> —WILLIAM GRAHAM SUMNER

WITH THE EXPULSION of Bao Dai in 1955 and the passing of the
deadline for a national plebiscite in 1956, the independent government of South Vietnam came to be accepted, like the
government of North Vietnam, as a permanent and sovereign
nation. While South Vietnam boasted a president and a parliament, its government was actually very much a family affair. The
family involved was the powerful Ngo clan from the city of Hué.
Ngo Dinh Diem was president, Ngo Dinh Thuc was the Catholic
archbishop of Hué, Ngo Dinh Nhu was the intellectual power
behind President Diem, and Ngo Dinh Nhu's energetic wife,
Madame Nhu, constituted herself a sort of personal roving ambassador of the family abroad. Ngo Dinh Can, the "founder of the
family's power," ruled in Hué itself.

These Ngo brothers were the children of a great Catholic mandarin, Ngo Dinh Kha; the fact of his being both a Catholic and a
mandarin effectively underlines the strange mixture of ideologies
with which he reared his sons. The Ngos were at once fervent
Catholics (their Catholicism, stemming from French missionary

efforts in the nineteenth century, was, according to most observers, of a very much more fanatical kind than is typical of French Catholics) and fervent nationalists. But the Ngo family nationalism stemmed from the antagonism of the mandarin class to French usurpation of their prerogatives; it had nothing to do with socialism, liberalism, or any of the other political ideals that have inspired national liberation movements in former colonies. Ngo Dinh Nhu himself was a graduate of France's École des Chartes, and in his mastery of various French intellectual currents for the purpose of expelling French power from Vietnam, he typified the contradictions inherent in the family outlook.

For if the Ngo family's Catholicism was fanatical, it was deeply influenced by the traditional Vietnamese reliance on the family, stemming from the age-old "true religion" of Vietnam: ancestor worship. And if the family was deeply nationalistic, its nationalism was for a Vietnam that would return to past traditions of hierarchy and authoritarianism. Of course the Ngos' religious convictions made them bitter and sworn foes of communism, supplying them with not only an established anti-Communist philosophy, but one rooted in fervent faith. That the Catholicism of the Ngos was something peculiar to their family was indicated again and again by the conflicts that developed between Archbishop Ngo Dinh Thuc and the Vatican's representative in Vietnam, the Archbishop of Saigon, Monsignor Binh.

As we have seen, Vietnamese Catholics, although numbering almost two million, remained a small minority when compared to other religious groups in the nation, especially the Buddhists. Yet Vietnamese society has always been exceptionally tolerant in religious matters, and the Catholic minority, especially since it represented those who had adopted at least this much of French civilization, had prospered. How it would fare when the Ngo family attempted to make it supreme in Vietnam was another matter.

With the final withdrawal of French forces from South Vietnam during 1955 and 1956, President Diem was faced with massive problems. The most dangerous of these was undoubtedly the existence of several well-armed religious-political sects within the country. Three of these, the Cao-Dai, the Hoa-Hao and the

Binh-Xuyen, maintained private armies, secret party organizations
and the allegiance of thousands of followers. The Cao-Dai sect
was based on a fusion of Buddhism, Christian teachings and
humanism; it had been favored by Admiral D'Argenlieu as a possible counter to the Vietminh. The French had turned over
several provinces of South Vietnam to the Cao-Daists, who maintained their own administration, their own finances and their own
armed forces. The Hoa-Hao sect, taking its name from that of the
village in which it was born, was smaller, but had control of various
rice markets in western South Vietnam. Its founder, Huynh Phu
So, was both a Buddhist mystic and a socialist. At times allying
himself with the Vietminh, he came to be known as the "mad
bonze" and was eventually executed by the Vietminh. The seven
or eight thousand members of the Hoa-Hao sect vacillated between cooperation with the Vietminh and with Diem's regime.
Perhaps the best armed and most ruthless of these sects was the
Binh-Xuyen, originally another semireligious group that had degenerated into a gang of river pirates who under the French were
used to staff the Saigon police force.

The Cao-Dai, the Hoa-Hao and the Binh-Xuyen had all been
encouraged by the French, not only because of their more or less
anti-Vietminh stance, but also as a means of splitting nationalist
sentiment in South Vietnam. The sects, in turn, while cooperating with the French, did not hesitate to cooperate also with the
Japanese during World War II. So great was their power that no
government could effectively rule in South Vietnam until they
had been eliminated, or at least disarmed. Diem moved against
the sects during 1955, and in several sharp battles he succeeded
at least in expelling them (especially the Binh-Xuyen) from Saigon. All of which might have been totally praiseworthy had not
Diem's move been actuated as much by religious as political considerations. While the Binh-Xuyen were little better than gang-
sters, and few mourned their passing, the Cao-Dai and Hoa-Hao
groups commanded the respect of millions of Vietnamese as
being religiously inspired. Diem's campaign against them therefore smacked of religious persecution to very many South
Vietnamese.

The regime Diem established in South Vietnam was severe and

dictatorial. Political opponents of whatever stripe were branded
Communists and dispatched to concentration camps, where
many were tortured and many perished. The excuse offered for
this policy was that any opponent of the Diem government,
whether he intended to or not, could only be playing into the
hands of the Vietminh, now, of course, transformed into the government of North Vietnam. Although no actual state of war
existed between the two halves of Vietnam, it was assumed by
Diem and his followers that conflict was a continuing and inevitable fact.

In this Diem was not altogether wrong, yet it is difficult to tell
just where the chain of action and reaction began. It will be
recalled that in 1954 about five thousand Vietminh local leaders
had stayed behind in South Vietnam, burying their arms and
communications equipment and adopting the role of peaceful
peasants, awaiting the 1956 elections. In the cities, Vietminh
stay-behinds had organized a Committee of Peace, headed by
Nguyen Huu Tho, a non-Communist. This committee had been
banned and its leaders, including Nguyen Huu Tho, imprisoned.
A few months after the passing of the date set at Geneva for reunification elections, the Vietminh leaders in the countryside began
a campaign of murdering local village chiefs. They selected for
assassination chiefs who had either been sent out by the Saigon
government (and therefore had no deep ties with their villages)
or those whose conduct had earned them the hatred of local peasants. The intention obviously was to destroy the Diem government's links with the countryside. Nor is it certain whether this
early campaign of rural terror was undertaken at the behest of the
North Vietnamese government (or even with their knowledge
and approval) or whether it was a spontaneous reaction of frustra-
tion and rage against Diem's refusal to permit the long-awaited
elections. In any event, by 1957 such terrorist tactics were not un-
common, and Diem could well believe he was faced with armed
revolt.

Diem's response to terrorism was to institute terrorism of his
own. Not only were concentration camps used; Vietnamese Army
patrols began prowling the countryside to root out and execute
the rebels. They were, however, faced with the same all-but-insol-

uble problem that had confounded the French and was later to confound the Americans: how could one tell who, among the peasants, was a rebel and who was not? Informers among the villagers might point accusing fingers, but suppose these informers were merely accusing people they wished to see eliminated for personal reasons? And as rural terrorism increased, informers grew fewer; it was dangerous to "turn in" a rebel: his comrades would certainly take vengeance. Faced with such difficulties, impatient officers in charge of the army patrols, under pressure from their superiors to "show results," increasingly turned to haphazard arrests, torture and executions with or without evidence that the people they shot were actually guilty of anything. Of course this desperate policy only increased peasant hatred of the Diem regime and all its works—which was precisely the aim for which the rebels were striving. Thus Diem's counterterror was truly counterproductive.

But even without rebel terror and government counterterror in the countryside, the policies of the Diem government produced increasingly wide opposition among the South Vietnamese people. No real land-reform policy was undertaken; instead, taxes were increased and landlords confirmed in their possessions. While some real progress, under American stimulation, was made in such fields as education (the number of grade-school pupils was doubled between 1955 and 1960; the number of secondary-school pupils increased fivefold), the old class structure of society was not modified. The poor in South Vietnam not only remained poor (as indeed they did in North Vietnam), but they continued to be confronted (as they were not in North Vietnam) by the spectacle of the pleasures of the very rich. If, with American economic aid, cities were modernized, highways improved, port facilities enlarged, the vast mass of the South Vietnamese people did not enjoy any change in their poverty-stricken standard of living. It seemed that only the rich, the government officials and the army benefited from all this. And when unionists or other groups in Saigon, Hué or other cities organized peaceful protests for higher wages, shorter hours, more equitable taxation, they were met by the police or the army. Protest under the Diem government was answered by prison and bullets.

There was little doubt, too, that the continuing presence of the

American Military Advisor Group, however small, combined with the tremendously increased "sense" of an American presence in South Vietnam due to the distribution and administration of American aid, increasingly irritated the always strong nationalism of the people. The French were gone, true—but had not the Americans come to take their place? And even if there were no American forces present, it was well known that the American government fully supported the Diem regime, a fact that earned the United States increasing distrust and even hatred among the very people it was attempting to help. Diem claimed to be a patriot, but was he not "selling out" to a new foreign master?

All of these were the irreducible circumstances that enmeshed the government of the Ngos. But these circumstances themselves arose from the fact that both the Ngos and their American supporters were victims of doctrine. Their decisions, their actions, their justifications proceeded from and were judged in the light of doctrine. Not only interpretations but facts were twisted to fit preconceived ideas. For the Ngos, the central doctrine of which they were prisoners began with the assumption that communism as an economic-political philosophy was an absolute evil and that all its adherents were absolutely evil people, or, at best, absolutely misled people following absolutely evil leaders. Any means to combat this evil were automatically justified. Anyone who doubted the wisdom of any government policy was either a Communist or a Communist dupe. Since the Ngos were certain of their own anti-Communist integrity, anyone who questioned either their aims or their means was morally guilty of aiding and/or abetting absolute evil. And where absolutes were concerned there was no possibility of compromise, no room for disagreement. The Ngo regime in South Vietnam turned into something very like a Fascist police state, except that its atmosphere was more medieval than radical. To combat the present menace of communism, the Ngos summoned all that was authoritarian from the distant Vietnamese past.

While not actuated by questions of moral evil, the Americans were, during the late 1950s, also gripped by doctrine. Their doctrine began with the assumption that world communism was an unchanging, monolithic whole, bent on the fastest possible exter-

mination of the non-Communist world. Each and every branch of
this entirety was, despite national differences, essentially an extension of a central will to world conquest. Communism was viewed
as an octopus whose tentacles in eastern Europe, in Korea, in the
Far East and in Vietnam were directed from Moscow and Peking.
To prevent those tentacles from enlarging the area of Communist
domination was to frustrate the central will behind them; eventually, deprived of new conquest, that will to power would die
and then the internal structure of the Communist world would
either change or collapse. Thus it was assumed that Ho Chi
Minh's government in North Vietnam was merely the puppet of
Moscow and Peking; it was further assumed that the insurgents
in South Vietnam were creatures of Ho's regime. Thus, no matter
how distasteful the Ngo government might grow, to support it
against its own rebels and critics was to strike a blow against
communism throughout the world.

    To what extent did these doctrines square with actuality? First
of all, leaving aside religiously inspired moral philosophy, what
kind of state had come into being in North Vietnam, that area
north of the 17th parallel from which, according to both Saigon
and Washington, danger threatened? The government erected by
Ho and his followers was certainly authoritarian in the Communist tradition. Although non-Communists were accorded places
in the government, no rival political party was tolerated. The
press, the radio and other means of communication were strictly
controlled. The largest industries, especially mining, transportation and public utilities, were nationalized. This meant the dispossession not only of foreign (primarily French) owners, but
also of Vietnamese. On the other hand, a relatively large sector,
including small businesses, shops, etc., was left to private owner-
ship. Although more heavily industrialized than the south, North
Vietnam was far from being industrialized enough to adopt an
all-out socialist economy. Instead, for the time being, a mixed
economy was encouraged. And in this essentially peasant country,
a drastic land-reform program was undertaken. This meant the
dispossession of thousands of Vietnamese landlords (who were
often accused of being "feudalists" and brought to trial before
village "juries" that imposed harsh sentences) and the redistribu-

tion of their land to formerly landless peasants. As the social structure of the Vietnamese countryside was based on the village unit rather than the individual or family, in practice, land reform generally meant that villages simply no longer paid rent for the land they had long tilled. Instead they would henceforth pay government taxes, but at least for these they were receiving schools, hospitals, improved roads, etc. Proceeding with customary caution, Ho's government did not collectivize the land or establish a "state farm" system such as that prevalent in Russia. In short, North Vietnam, though following a pattern of socialist development, had by no means reached the stage at which even its economy might be described as "Communist."

In dealing with dissidents, the North Vietnamese government showed itself no less stern, in some respects, than that of South Vietnam. When the land-reform program was pressed too rapidly during 1956 in the province of Nghe-Trinh (the birthplace, it will be recalled, of the first "Xo-Viets" in 1930), certain elements of the population rose in rebellion. They were harshly suppressed by the army—and in 1960 officials in Hanoi would admit that many of those "liquidated" at the time had probably been innocent. A year later, in 1957, certain North Vietnamese scholars, teachers and lower-level government officials rebelled against the government's programs. This so-called Intellectuals' Revolt was also put down none too gently. Yet through all these travails, the average North Vietnamese, more concerned (as were his southern brethren) with his immediate daily food, shelter and labor than with abstract principles of democracy, personal liberty and equal justice, could see all about him and experience in his personal life solid evidence of material progress. More than that, he was convinced (as his southern brethren were not) that the government in Hanoi truly had his interests at heart. So whatever one may think of the doctrine that equates communism with absolute evil, it certainly had no relevance to reality in North Vietnam, especially not to the population of that country which continued to revere "Uncle" Ho and his chief lieutenants, General Giap and Pham Van Dong.

But what of Ho's links to the world Communist movement? Certainly North Vietnam continued to receive material and diplomatic support from both the Soviet Union and Red China. And in that simple statement lies the clue to a very important anachronism. For in 1956 Russian dictator Joseph Stalin died. Within a very short time his heirs had started quarreling with Mao Tse-tung's regime in China; soon the quarrel became so bitter that the possibility of war between the two giants of the Communist world could not be dismissed. Yet Ho continued to receive aid from both of these now-mortal enemies. In order to do so he had to very carefully refrain from taking sides in their dispute. That is to say, neither China nor Russia, as it turned out, swung enough weight in Hanoi to compel Ho to join either against the other. In this respect it is necessary to recall the ancient Vietnamese distrust and fear of China, the fact that Ho's domestic policies did not by any means meet with the unqualified approval of the theorists of either Moscow or Peking, and the stubbornly nationalistic streak in the Vietnamese Communist movement that had made it possible for Ho to cooperate even with the detested French and Americans when Vietnamese *national* interests so dictated. The view of North Vietnam as merely another tentacle of a world Communist aggression was as false as similar views of Yugoslavia, for example, had proved to be. In fact, North Vietnamese independence of both Moscow and Peking was in direct proportion to how much aid North Vietnam required—which in turn was proportioned directly by how much military pressure was exerted against it by the United States. Only Washington could force North Vietnam into greater dependence on Moscow and Peking, thus making the American doctrine a self-fulfilling prophecy perhaps, but not, before 1960, a fact.

But what of the insurgency in South Vietnam after 1956, sponsored and nourished, claimed Ngo Dinh Diem, by the Communist north? Were the rebels really North Vietnamese agents? Was their program of selective terror in the countryside an act of covert North Vietnamese aggression? To answer these complicated questions, one must bear in mind that to the Vietnamese, following the Geneva settlements, Vietnam remained *one nation.* The Vietminh forces that had defeated the French had been drawn from all sections of the country; Ho Chi Minh's guerrilla war had been nationwide. The Vietminh cadres left behind in South Vietnam after 1954 did not look upon themselves as North Vietnamese agents. They looked upon themselves as Vietminh veterans and adherents to the Vietnamese Communist Party directed by Ho Chi Minh who were simply awaiting the reunification of their country in 1956, at which time free elections would decide the composition of a national government. These veterans did not begin to act until late in 1956, long after the date for those elections had passed. The tempo of their actions did not reach serious proportions until 1958, when it was perfectly apparent that Diem had no intention of permitting reunification. At this time the repressive nature of his American-supported regime also became clear. While there can be little doubt that North Vietnam, through propaganda, lent moral support to the insurgents in the south and permitted supplies to be smuggled to them from time to time, the sequence of events strongly suggests that the guerrilla warfare confronting the Diem regime was not "aggression from the north" but an inevitable domestic response to conditions in South Vietnam.

It was in March 1960 that a group of Vietminh veterans in eastern Quang Ngai province (about sixty miles south of the 17th parallel) began to operate on a very organized basis. They issued a proclamation describing the situation in South Vietnam under the Diem regime as "intolerable" and calling for nationwide insurrection. Nguyen Huu Tho, the non-Communist president of the Committee of Peace (one of the suppressed reunification organizations that flourished briefly after 1954), sent these veterans a letter urging them to act. Tho himself was at that time imprisoned by the Diem government near Saigon. This defiant "call to arms" was noted by the government of North Vietnam, and for the first time since 1954 Ho Chi Minh's regime announced publicly that it would not abandon its allies in the south. In December 1960, at a meeting of about one hundred "underground" delegates held "somewhere in South Vietnam," the National Liberation Front (NLF) was born. The NLF, or Viet Cong, announced itself as a broadly based resistance movement with a ten-point program moderate enough to enlist the support of democrats and nationalists as well as Communists. Its leader was to be Nguyen Huu Tho, whose escape from Diem's prisons was engineered by Viet Cong agents in December 1961.

But despite the emergence of the Viet Cong in 1960, the Diem

regime in South Vietnam faced even graver and more immediate
dangers than the growing guerrilla war in the countryside. On
November 11, 1960, for example, several units of South Vietnamese paratroopers rebelled against Diem and encircled his
palace in Saigon. Only the rebels' hesitation prevented their success; they were disarmed by loyal troops. But this defiance of the
Diem government by some of its elite units showed how brittle
Diem's power had become.

It was early in 1961 that the new American President, John F.
Kennedy, decided that if South Vietnam was to be preserved both
from unification with the north and from its own Viet Cong insurgents, an entirely new approach would be needed. Several fact-
finding missions were dispatched to Saigon during the summer of
1961, and one of them, headed by Professor Eugene Staley of the
Stanford Research Institute, worked out a new overall war plan
to defeat the Viet Cong. The key to this plan was the "strategic
hamlet" concept. The theory behind it was both to cut the Viet
Cong off from contact with the rural population and to protect
that population from Viet Cong reprisals and terrorism. Around
already existing rural cities and larger towns, new hamlets,
guarded by bamboo hedges and watchtowers manned by government troops, were to be set up. Villagers working in the fields
during the day could retire to these hamlets at night. If Communist doctrine had long since described guerrillas as "fish" swim-
ming in the "water" (the rural population), then the "Staley
Formula" would deprive the fish of their natural habitat.

But in attempting this drastic alteration of Vietnamese village
life the Diem government was touching on the very foundations
of Vietnamese existence. For in Vietnam, as has been observed,
the village and not the individual was the basic social unit. Everything derived from the village, and even individual private life
was based on the village structure. The strategic hamlet concept
attacked this basic social unit ruthlessly, disrupting old ties, up-
setting old customs and imposing a totally new and unwelcome
social pattern on people whose intimate village society had not
been basically disturbed for centuries. While Diem justified this
"revolution" in the countryside as a means of combating the
Viet Cong "enemy," most rural Vietnamese simply did not consider the Viet Cong guerrillas as "enemies." Rather, they thought

of them as dangerous brothers engaged in a frightening but comprehensible rebellion against increasing oppression. The strategic hamlet program therefore only earned Diem the hatred of those (about ten percent of the rural population) whose lives were disrupted by it. Furthermore, and perhaps of even deeper significance, it frightened the traditionalist leadership of Vietnam's greatest religious sect, the Buddhists.

Ever since the Diem regime had established itself in 1954, South Vietnam's Buddhist monks, the "bonzes," had sensed increasing persecution. The power and vitality of the Catholic minority in South Vietnam had grown with the influx of Catholic refugees from the north, and the Diem family seized every opportunity to strengthen Catholic influence throughout South Vietnamese society. Diem's government looked upon the Buddhists as automatically a part of the "opposition" and treated them accordingly. Although, before 1963, not badly persecuted, the Buddhists were discriminated against, viewed with suspicion and treated with contempt. In turn many Vietnamese saw in Buddhism a means of defying the unpopular Diem regime. By joining the Buddhists one could demonstrate one's anti-Diem convictions in a reasonably safe way. Yet Buddhism was not, nor could it ever be, a politically oriented movement. Bonze Sobhita has described it:

"Buddhism properly speaking is not a religion, in the sense that it does not recognize God or soul, and has no dogma. The practice of Buddhism is the search for a conduct that will permit a person to cut short the cycle of re-births, to destroy desire and, along that road, arrive at Nirvana—which is not annihilation but a state between being and non-being, extinction, appeasement of desires, peace and serenity.

"For Buddhism the world itself does not exist: there is no beginning or end: there are only transitory phenomena whose origins are interdependent: all is tied together by the law of causality. This law of causality is the result of our actions. Added to our past life, this life serves our future life. The world is a dynamic world in a perpetual state of becoming, and man is only a succession of psychic states following each other from one body to the next. Death gives birth to another individual."

Hardly the doctrine of political activism. And to underscore that point, one of Vietnam's most prestigious bonzes, the Venerable Thich Tri Quang, explained in a magazine article written in 1958 that no person or government could ever mobilize Buddhism for any war, hot or cold; that Buddhism was, *par excellence*, the religion of *neutralism*. Yet this neutralism was precisely what the embattled Diem regime could neither understand nor forgive. To the fanatic Ngo family all who were not actively committed to the government were automatically against it. In treating Buddhists as "the enemy" the Diem government made them the enemy, forced them to take action. But the action Buddhists were to take would be unique to their religion and philosophy.

Many petty discriminations against the Buddhists culminated in the spring of 1963 when the Diem government decided to forbid any public ceremony in honor of Buddha's anniversary—despite the fact that the installation of Catholic bishops and the anniversary of Archbishop Ngo Dinh Thuc were always celebrated by large processions. On May 8, 1963, a large mass of Buddhists assembled outside the old imperial palace in Hué to protest this discrimination. Although the protesters were orderly, the military commander lost his head and ordered his troops to open fire on the assemblage. Eight people, including women and children, died under the soldiers' guns; many more were badly wounded.

A few weeks later, to protest this government atrocity, a Buddhist bonze, the Venerable Duc, seated himself outside the parliament building in Saigon, poured gasoline over his body and transformed himself into a human torch. From June to November 1963 seven more bonzes were to burn themselves to death publicly in witness against the Diem government. This was the "political action" suitable to the teachings of Buddha available to the Buddists of South Vietnam. It seemed utterly ineffective. Madame Nhu expressed what were no doubt the sentiments of the entire Ngo family when she remarked in August 1963: "I would clap hands at seeing another monk barbecue show. . . ."

But Madame Nhu was, to say the least, out of touch with world opinion. The flaming suicides of the Buddhist monks aroused horror everywhere and dramatically illuminated the excesses and repressions of the Ngo family dictatorship in Vietnam. American public opinion was aroused by these tragic suicides in such a

FAMILY PORTRAIT: *President Ngo Dinh Diem stands second from left; on his right stands brother Ngo Dinh Nhu, on his left brother Ngo Dinh Thuc, Archbishop of Hué. Madame Nhu poses fourth from right.*

A Buddhist nun burns herself alive in Hué while a watching bonze prays for an end to "Diemocracy."

way as to confirm the distaste with which President Kennedy and
his closest advisors had always viewed their forced association
with the Diem government. That distaste had grown to exaspera-
tion over the years as evidence of the misuse of American financial
and military aid had piled up. It had grown to alarm as evidence
had accumulated that Diem could not suppress the Viet Cong or
probably even preserve his own government in power. By 1963 it
had become apparent in Washington that the Ngo family could
not be the instrument with which the United States hoped to
achieve its ends in Vietnam—in fact, "Diemocracy" had become
an outright political liability.

Accordingly, when certain representatives of the South Vietnamese armed forces made cautious inquiries at the American
embassy in Saigon and among American officers of the Military
Advisory Group, American indifference to the fate of the Diem
regime was made clear to them. How deeply some American
officials may have been implicated in what happened next cannot
be determined as yet; certainly, both on instructions from Washington and as a reflection of their own feelings, American representatives in South Vietnam did nothing to discourage the downfall
of the Diem government.

With, therefore, the understanding that the Americans would
not interfere, a group of Vietnamese military officers undertook
to overthrow the Diem regime. Once again, it was the South Vietnamese paratroopers who provided the firepower, but this time
they succeeded. On November 1, 1963, the presidential palace in
Saigon was surrounded by paratrooper units. At 11 A.M. on that
day American Ambassador Henry Cabot Lodge presented himself
there and told Diem that his personal safety and that of his family,
as well as the interests of the country, demanded that he resign
the presidency. But Diem, and his brother Ngo Dinh Nhu, also
present at the palace, dismissed this suggestion. At about 2 P.M.
the paratroopers opened fire with machine guns and rifles. Seven
hours later, emissaries from the military revolutionary committee
undertaking the rebellion entered the palace to talk to Diem.
What they discussed has never been disclosed, but without further shooting, on the following day, November 2, 1963, Diem
and his brother left the palace in a private car. They found refuge

in the Catholic church of Saint François Xavier outside Saigon. A few moments later an armored half-track arrived. At 9:20 A.M. Ngo Dinh Diem and Ngo Dinh Nhu were hustled out of the church and into the half-track. An hour later Saigon radio announced that the two brothers had "committed suicide." Subsequent information confirmed that in fact they had been executed. Another brother, Ngo Dinh Can, sought refuge in the American consulate in Saigon, but two days later, under siege by angry crowds, the American consul surrendered Can to the new military authorities; six months later they executed him. Archbishop Thuc happened to be in Rome at the time, Madame Nhu in the United States. The Ngo family power in South Vietnam had been shattered; "Diemocracy" had come to an end.

CLOSE-UP

Two Letters Home

THE FOLLOWING letter, written by J. David Kinzie, an American doctor working in the Quang Ngai hospital in South Vietnam, was published in the magazine *Progressive* on March 15, 1965:

"I have been in Quang Ngai for six months in general practice at a civilian provincial hospital, and I can remain silent no longer.

"There comes a time in a doctor's life no matter how hardened he has become, and perhaps in every man's life no matter how cynical he may be, when he must protest as effectively as he can about the sufferings of his fellow man. When one's own country is involved in the inhumanity, the responsibility becomes greater. Thus I add my belated voice.

"The civilian hospital in our province in central Vietnam is good by Vietnamese standards. The patients, already diseased by tuberculosis, anemia, and malnutrition in many cases, are now entering more frequently from direct effects of the war. For example, a pregnant woman demonstrator with a bullet hole in her abdomen, whose fetus died later; a twelve-year-old boy brought in unconscious by relatives who described how artillery blasted their village the night before; a fifty-year-old woman accused of being Viet Cong who had been beaten, electrically shocked, and had her hands punctured for three days to extort information; three other civilians also accused of supporting the Viet Cong were released to the hospital after severe beatings and their innocence determined. Many of the victims' 'crimes' consisted merely in living in an area the Viet Cong had overrun the night before. . . .

"Of course war has always been described as evil, but does this mean that America must add to it? Our military advisors teach Vietnamese modern techniques of killing each other. Our weapons aid in more thorough destruction of themselves. Rather than liberating a people, it seems that these techniques and weapons result in innocent civilians, women and children being beaten, burned and murdered. . . .

"Is America to survive on the blood of Vietnamese civilians? Does this make us great?"

This child's mother has had her wounds bandaged. The child's wounds do not show.

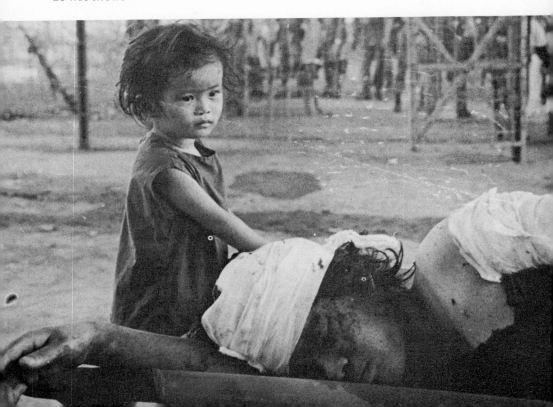

The following letter was written to his mother by United States Marine Corporal Ronnie Wilson of Wichita, Kansas:

"Mom, I had to kill a woman and a baby . . . We were searching the dead Cong when the wife of the one I was checking ran out of a cave. . . . I shot her and my rifle is automatic so before I knew it I had shot about six rounds. Four of them hit her and the others went into the cave and must have bounced off the rock wall and hit the baby. Mom, for the first time I felt really sick to my stomach. The baby was about two months old. I swear to God this place is worse than hell. Why must I kill women and kids? Who knows who's right? They think they are and we think we are. Both sides are losing men. I wish to God this was over."

Chapter Nine

AMERICANIZING THE WAR

> If this great nation is to be humiliated, is to be
> defeated . . . by that little nation, then I wish
> Red China would come in. It would be a great
> humiliation for this nation to be defeated by a
> small nation of 16 million people. If we must be
> be defeated, it would be better to lose to a large
> nation of 700 million people.
> —SENATOR RUSSELL LONG

WHEN JOHN FITZGERALD KENNEDY assumed the presidency in
January 1961, he inherited from the outgoing Eisenhower administration the American involvement in Southeast Asia. He was
also heir to the policies, plans and permanent level of Central
Intelligence Agency and military advisors who do not change with
elections. Although, as we have seen, there had never been a
public American pledge or commitment, except under very strictly
defined conditions, to engage American forces in South Vietnam,
Kennedy and his advisors felt the weight of a "moral" commitment that involved American prestige. The early 1960s were a
time of world crisis between the United States and the Soviet
Union; at Berlin, in Laos, and ultimately in Cuba, the two superpowers approached the brink of nuclear war. In his confrontation
with Soviet Premier Nikita Khrushchev, Kennedy felt that to
retreat in one area might invite aggression in other areas: a loss of
American prestige in Southeast Asia might entail a weakening of
the American "image" in Berlin and throughout the world. Thus,
although with private reservations as to how effective any Ameri-

can policy of force could be in the distant jungles of South Vietnam on the very fringes of Red China, the new American President never questioned the necessity of maintaining the American presence there. The question was: how should that presence be maintained?

President Eisenhower and Secretary of State John Foster Dulles, with the enthusiastic support of the United States Air Force, if not of the Army and Navy, had, during their years in office, adopted the policy known as "massive retaliation." According to this plan, while the United States might supply military advisors and equipment as well as financial support to nations threatened by Communist subversion or aggression, there would be no need to commit American ground, air or naval forces directly. For having drawn an imaginary line beyond which the expansion of communism would not be tolerated, the Eisenhower administration threatened total nuclear war upon Russia and/or China should such an expansion take place. This policy, it was hoped, would deter Communist aggression and lessen the burdens of maintaining a large defense establishment throughout the world.

The trouble with the policy of "massive retaliation" was that to be effective it had to be credible. Soviet and Red Chinese leaders had to believe that if, say, once again Chinese "volunteers" poured over the border of South Korea, then the United States Strategic Air Command would drop hydrogen bombs on Peking, Shanghai, and, in the event of Soviet intervention, Moscow and Leningrad. But as the thermonuclear and intercontinental ballistic missile armaments of the Soviet Union increased, this would mean a Soviet counterstrike against the United States. Would any American President risk the total destruction of his country for the sake of preserving the American presence in some distant and strategically unimportant area like South Korea? It seemed increasingly unlikely, not only to Communist governments, but also to such Allied governments as that of France, which proceeded to develop its own nuclear potential precisely because French President Charles de Gaulle had no confidence that the United States would commit national suicide to protect foreign nations.

And if, by 1961, the theory of "massive retaliation" had become incredible in terms of its use against outright aggression, it bore almost no relevance whatsoever to subversion. No one in the world believed that the United States would bring on a nuclear holocaust as a response to insurgency and subversion in Southeast Asia, or, for that matter, anywhere else in the world. The Kennedy administration was therefore faced with the task of developing a means of responding effectively to "wars of national liberation," native rebellions and Communist-inspired and -backed civil wars.

In an effort to find some way out of the morass in South Vietnam that would preserve the independence of that nation and yet limit American involvement in the growing guerrilla war there, Kennedy dispatched several fact-finding missions to Saigon during the summer of 1961. Vice-President Lyndon Johnson headed one such mission, General Maxwell Taylor another. Both reported that only a large increase in American aid and the commitment of American ground forces could preserve the Ngo Dinh Diem government. The United States Joint Chiefs of Staff also urged that American ground and naval forces be deployed. But Kennedy refused to go so far.

Instead he adopted a twofold policy designed to meet several problems at once. First of all, the theory and policy of "massive retaliation" were quietly dropped in favor of a policy of developing American ability to respond to limited aggression or subversion with limited force. The army and navy and the use of tactical rather than strategic air power were the key elements of this new policy. The nuclear missiles remained in their silos, of course, but highly air-mobile smaller "normal" forces with greatly increased firepower were developed to deal with "brush-fire" wars. And an entirely new "counterinsurgency" force was created to deal with situations of Communist-backed subversion. This force, headed by the new Special Forces unit, the "Green Berets," was composed of highly trained specialists in jungle and guerrilla warfare. The Green Berets were intended to train and lead local village militias against the Viet Cong insurgents. At the same time Kennedy recognized, as Eisenhower and Dulles had not, that any American effort in South Vietnam was doomed to failure unless the Vietnamese people themselves were willing to fight for their independence. This in turn entailed the reformation of the Diem regime in Saigon.

On December 15, 1961, President Kennedy elaborated the new American policy in Vietnam in a letter to Ngo Dinh Diem. The Military Assistance and Advisory Group in Saigon was to be expanded (from about 2,000 men in 1961 to 15,000 men in 1963). American logistical support teams and tactical air combat and helicopter teams would be sent, and several hundred of the new Green Berets would be committed to the jungle fighting. At the same time, Diem would have to reform his government in such a way as to win the support of the South Vietnamese people. It was very obvious that by increasing the American military presence and support in South Vietnam in the way he did, President Kennedy hoped to head off the need for any massive American combat commitment before it became necessary.

As we have seen, however, the government of Ngo Dinh Diem did not reform itself (instead it launched vitriolic newspaper attacks on Americans who suggested reform), nor did it ever enlist the sympathies of the South Vietnamese people in its anti-Communist crusade. On the contrary, it developed into an authoritarian dictatorship, and the only way the Kennedy administration could have prevented that would have been by dispatching massive American ground forces to Vietnam, precisely the action Kennedy hoped to avoid. When Diem was assassinated and his regime overthrown in November 1963, the way was cleared for a new policy in South Vietnam, but what President Kennedy's response to that might have been would never be known. For three weeks after Diem's downfall, Kennedy himself was assassinated in Dallas. His successor, Lyndon Johnson, was one of those, it will be remembered, who had urged the use of American ground forces in Vietnam in 1961.

The fall of the Ngo family's dictatorship in South Vietnam did not usher in a period of political stability and democracy. The military junta that had toppled Diem, through its leader, General Duong Van "Big" Minh, hastened to announce that it would relinquish power to a truly democratic civilian government in "the very near future." Unfortunately, however, the military men could not seem to agree on what would constitute such a government. As a result, one after another of the South Vietnamese generals emerged as the "strongman" in Saigon during the next few years. While parliamentary elections were held and civilian ministers came and went, it grew painfully apparent that real power in South Vietnam was to remain in the hands of the military. Until 1965 the only real changes in that power were to be the names of the military men who held it. In that year South Vietnamese Air Force General Nguyen Cao Ky established himself as chief of state with a regime as dictatorial as ever Diem's had been. Furthermore, as a refugee from North Vietnam, General Ky was an advocate of the invasion of the north.

With the fall of Diem and the passing of political power into the hands of a rotating series of military "strongmen," the independent political life of South Vietnam may be said to have, to all intents and purposes, come to an end. Only continued and increasing American support (or the threat to withhold it) now really influenced the policies and leadership of South Vietnamese governments. And the Americans, perforce, were faced with one overriding question: was the current "strongman," the current regime, a useful instrument for the carrying out of American policy in South Vietnam? If not, the regime would fall. For after the death of President Kennedy, American policy in Vietnam underwent a series of dramatic changes. And each step in this series was accompanied by the fall of one set of South Vietnamese military rulers and the emergence of another, culminating in the coming to power of the "all-out war" advocate, General Nguyen Cao Ky.

If the fall of the Diem regime was greeted in North Vietnam as the inevitable consequence of its failures, in South Vietnam it seemed to presage the early victory of the Viet Cong. If, after all, the government of South Vietnam was so weak, so little supported by its own people that it could be overthrown by its own generals (and with tacit American acceptance of that overthrow), then it seemed that only the National Liberation Front offered a real alternative. Besides, Viet Cong military successes multiplied during 1964. Diem's strategic hamlets, built by the thousands, were destroyed or captured by the Viet Cong by the thousands. The

assassination of village chiefs and leaders reached such proportions
that few Vietnamese could be found who were willing to accept
such positions. Viet Cong-controlled territory increased to the
point where only the large cities and their immediate environs
could be considered relatively "secure." South Vietnamese troops,
despite their American equipment and advisors, showed less and
less inclination to fight the Viet Cong guerrillas. Clearly, during
the summer of 1964, South Vietnam was in imminent danger of
total collapse.

What would be the American response? Nineteen sixty-four
was an American presidential election year. President Lyndon
Baines Johnson, Kennedy's heir, was campaigning against Senator
Barry Goldwater, the Republican nominee. Goldwater favored a
very aggressive American policy in Asia (indeed, throughout the
world) against communism. Intemperately he even allowed himself to be pictured as a trigger-happy candidate who might plunge
the world into nuclear war. President Johnson, on the other hand,
insisted on his "reasonable," "moderate" and "sane" policies
designed to achieve American aims without war. Yet, if some
crisis in Vietnam, some dramatic defeat for American policy there
seemed to indicate that Johnson was too "soft" in his policies, if
he could be pictured as an "appeaser," then Goldwater might use
effectively against him the charge that the Johnson administration
had "lost Vietnam," just as Dwight D. Eisenhower's supporters
had accused the Truman administration of "losing China." It
was a very taut political tightrope that President Johnson had to
tread during the summer of 1964. And the much-feared crisis in
Vietnam appeared on schedule.

On July 31, 1964, patrol torpedo boats of the South Vietnamese
Navy shelled two islands off the North Vietnamese coast. Hover-
ing nearby were two American destroyers, the *Maddox* and the
C. Turner Joy. Were they "covering" the South Vietnamese action? United States naval officials denied that. The destroyers
were on normal patrol duties and merely "happened" to be passing by at the time of the South Vietnamese shelling. On the other
hand, the destroyers were only eleven miles from the coast of
North Vietnam—and North Vietnam, like the Soviet Union and
many other nations (non-Communist as well as Communist),

claimed that her territorial limits extended twelve miles out to sea. It was admitted later that one of the reasons that the two destroyers were so close to the North Vietnamese coast was to demonstrate to North Vietnam that the United States did not recognize any nation's claim to a twelve-mile offshore territorial limit. Whether or not the United States would have been willing to send two destroyers close inshore to the Soviet Union to make the same demonstration was a question never asked. In any event, toward dusk, several North Vietnamese torpedo boats appeared. The *Maddox* and the *C. Turner Joy* promptly turned away from the coast and headed for the open sea. They reported that the North Vietnamese torpedo boats were firing at them but had scored no hits.

Four days later, at exactly 9:52 P.M. on August 4, the *Maddox* and the *C. Turner Joy* signaled that they were again under attack by North Vietnamese "naval units." They also reported that none of the torpedoes launched against them had struck home and that they were fighting a "defensive counterattack." At 10:15 P.M. the two ships radioed that they had sunk one of the enemy units but that "the darkness hampered their action." At midnight planes from the huge American aircraft carrier *Ticonderoga* attacked the North Vietnamese ships and sank two more.

Within twelve hours of this incident, President Johnson reported to the American people that United States Air Force and Navy planes had made heavy "reprisal" attacks against North Vietnamese port and naval facilities. Twenty-five North Vietnamese torpedo boats (about one-half of the North Vietnamese Navy) had been sunk in these attacks and fuel storage facilities destroyed. At the same time, the United States delegate to the United Nations, Adlai Stevenson, asked that body to "condemn unprovoked North Vietnamese aggression," while the Johnson administration asked Congress for a resolution supporting the use of American forces to "retaliate" against such attacks.

In the United Nations only Nationalist China and Britain supported the American resolution; in the Senate, debate was cautious. Senator Gaylord A. Nelson of Wisconsin wanted to know how close to the North Vietnamese coast the American ships had been at the time of the July 31 incident:

MR. FULBRIGHT: It was testified they went in at least eleven miles in order to show that we do not recognize a twelve-mile limit, which I believe North Vietnam has asserted.

MR. NELSON: The patrolling was for the purpose of demonstrating to the North Vietnamese that we did not recognize a twelve-mile limit?

MR. FULBRIGHT: That was one reason given. . . .

MR. NELSON: It would be mighty risky, if Cuban PT boats were firing on Florida, for Russian armed ships or destroyers to be patrolling between us and Cuba, eleven miles out.

Yet the legalities of the affair hardly mattered. According to international law and the charter of the United Nations, no nation had the right to stage "reprisal" raids into another's territory. Furthermore, the tremendous imbalance between the "provocation" and the American response to it seemed to make the very word "reprisal" irrelevant. Neither of the American destroyers had been damaged (in fact a single bullet scar on the *Maddox* was all the proof the U.S. Navy could muster that the attack had even taken place) and no American was injured. Yet more than sixty-four planes took part in the "reprisal" raids that devastated four North Vietnamese coastal cities.

"The world remembers, the world must never forget, that aggression unchallenged is aggression unleashed," President Johnson declared to the American people. But whose was the aggression? In any event, the United States Senate adopted a resolution authorizing the President to employ the United States armed forces at his discretion to repel or punish "aggression" in Vietnam.

The problem of how to identify from where the "aggression" came was underscored on November 1, 1964, when Viet Cong units mortared the American air base at Bien Hoa. Twenty U.S. Air Force planes were destroyed and seven Americans killed. On December 24, 1964, the Viet Cong bombed a hotel in Saigon that had been reserved for the use of American officers. Several died. These were clear-cut challenges: acts of war during a civil war. But instead of staging "reprisals" against the Viet Cong in South Vietnam, the Johnson administration decided to punish North Vietnam. American and South Vietnamese planes attacked the Dong Hoi region, about thirty miles north of the 17th parallel.

On February 1, 1965, the United States State Department released a "White Paper" on the situation in Vietnam. It stated:

"The hard core of the Communist forces attacking South Vietnam are men trained in North Vietnam. They are ordered into the south and remain under the military discipline of the Military High Command in Hanoi. . . .

"Thus, since 1959, nearly 20,000 VC officers, soldiers, and technicians are known to have entered South Vietnam under orders from Hanoi. . . .

"The [National] Liberation Front is Hanoi's creation; it is neither independent nor southern, and what it seeks is not the liberation but the subjugation of the south. . . ."

After offering proofs of North Vietnamese involvement in the struggle between the National Liberation Front and the Saigon government, the White Paper ended on an ominous note:

"The choice now between peace and continued and increasingly destructive conflict is one for the authorities in Hanoi to make."

This was a clear announcement that the United States was on the verge of escalating the war in Vietnam, of changing its terms. Thus far, despite massive American aid in supplies and a very large force of American "advisors" and Special Forces (the Green Berets), the United States had basically been helping the governments (which changed with alarming rapidity) of South Vietnam to fight a domestic guerrilla war. American action against North Vietnam had been justified only in terms of "reprisals" for North Vietnamese attacks on Americans. Now, Washington was making it clear that the United States was prepared to carry the war to North Vietnam without further provocation. In other words, to destroy the Viet Cong in South Vietnam, the United States would make war on North Vietnam. Some observers likened this policy to that of a man who, unable to crush the head of a bothersome snake, painted its tail red and tried to kill it by hacking away at the tail.

The steps in this change of American policy are worth pondering.

Before 1964, the United States had identified the enemy in

South Vietnam as the Viet Cong guerrillas. It had helped various Saigon regimes to combat these guerrillas.

During 1964, the United States had declared that the true enemy in South Vietnam was North Vietnam, but had refrained from attacking this enemy, except when provoked or in "reprisal."

Beginning in 1965, the United States declared that the only way to win the war in South Vietnam was to attack North Vietnam—the very fact that the guerrilla war continued being taken as "aggression" from the north, as a standing "provocation" that would be met by continuous "reprisal."

But before the next step in escalating the war would be taken, President Johnson offered his own proposals for peace. On April 7, 1965, speaking in Baltimore, the President outlined the American position, a position that may be summarized in four basic points:

1. The United States would agree to unconditional negotiations with North Vietnam.

2. The United States would not negotiate with the National Liberation Front in South Vietnam, because it regarded this group as merely puppets of Hanoi.

3. The American objective was to maintain the independence of South Vietnam, which would remain "neutral" in the ongoing Cold War between world communism and the western capitalist states.

4. The United States would be willing to spend a billion dollars in an economic development program that would include North as well as South Vietnam.

"We will not be defeated," President Johnson declared. "We will not grow tired. We will not withdraw, either openly or under the cloak of a meaningless agreement."

President Johnson's formula was foredoomed to failure. Whether or not the United States considered the Viet Cong to be under Hanoi's direct orders (and there was no evidence of this; on the contrary, the National Liberation Front in South Vietnam was touchily independent), the National Liberation Front certainly existed and was the prime enemy in South Vietnam. To refuse to negotiate with the N.L.F. was to refuse meaningful negotiations at all. As for "Mr. Johnson's Billion," as it came to be called, this generous offer was somewhat marred by the circumstances under which it was made. On February 8, 1965, the United States Air Force had commenced "round the clock" heavy bombing attacks on North Vietnam; North Vietnamese leaders could hardly be expected to accept American charity while American bombs rained down upon them.

Yet the response of Premier Pham Van Dong of North Vietnam to the American proposals was relatively mild. It was made as a policy statement on April 14, 1965, and basically called for a return to the principles set forth by the Geneva agreements. Pham Van Dong's four points for peace were:

1. The United States, in accordance with the Geneva agreements, must withdraw all its forces from South Vietnam, dismantle all its military bases there, cancel its military alliance with South Vietnam and refrain from making attacks on North Vietnam.

2. Pending the peaceful reunification of all Vietnam, the two military zones established at Geneva must be strictly respected. Neither side must join any military alliance with any foreign powers.

3. The internal affairs of South Vietnam must be settled by the South Vietnamese people themselves, in accordance with the program of the N.L.F., without any foreign interference.

4. The eventual peaceful reunification of Vietnam is to be settled by the Vietnamese people themselves in both zones, without any foreign interference.

The distance between these two positions seems to have been decisive for Washington. Already, on March 10, about 3,000 United States marines had been landed at Da Nang to establish there a huge American base in South Vietnam. Now the decision was made in Washington to follow these with a massive commitment of American ground forces. The mask of the Military Advisory Group was dropped as an American High Command was established in Saigon to take over the total direction of the war. Within two years of President Johnson's peace proposals, more than five hundred thousand American soldiers were fighting in

South Vietnam. The United States, without a declaration of war by Congress (the "Tonkin Bay Resolution" was deemed adequate by the administration), was embarked on that nightmare of every American military strategist since General Douglas MacArthur: a land war in Asia.

CLOSE-UP

Operation Ranch Hand

AT ONE CORNER of the huge American air base at Tan Son Nhut, South Vietnam, hidden behind an old hangar, is the headquarters of Ranch Hand, the U.S. Air Force defoliation operation. The pilots of Ranch Hand are all volunteers; they have to be, because their mission is very risky. They fly twin-prop Fairchild C-123 "Providers," lumbering transport planes that look as if they had just flown out of World War II. The C-123s of Ranch Hand have been re-equipped to spray 2-4D, a chemical compound deadly to all plant life.

Ranch Hand operates on a six-day week, flying two missions per day. A mission may last from forty minutes to two hours, depending on the target. By 1966 the men who flew Ranch Hand's seven planes had already earned twenty-seven Purple Hearts, largely because of their vulnerability to ground fire. The chemical defoliant must be sprayed from a height of 150 feet at a speed of 130 knots. At any higher altitude or faster speed, the spray does not settle on the foliage in sufficient strength. At a lower height the vegetation would be "overkilled," a waste of valuable chemicals. The average

11,000-pound load of 2-4D carried by each Ranch Hand plane costs about $5,000 and requires four minutes to spray. It will kill every growing thing over an area of 300 acres.

A 1,000-gallon chemical tank is carried inside the fuselage of the C-123 with tubing leading out to the spray nozzles. The pilot triggers the actual release of the chemical, while, in an armored compartment in the rear, the spray operator monitors the pump that forces the 2-4D out of its dispensing tubes. The average Ranch Hand mission sprays an area 10 miles long and 90 yards wide. When Ranch Hand planes encounter enemy antiaircraft fire (their slow speed, low altitude and lack of maneuverability make them particularly vulnerable targets, even for rifle fire) the spray operator tosses down a smoke grenade to indicate the source of the ground fire. This leads the fast jet Skyraiders who escort Ranch Hand missions to the target, which they then "suppress" with rockets and bombs.

Prime targets for Ranch Hand include the areas along highways and railroads to make it more difficult for the Viet Cong to ambush convoys. The perimeters of Special Forces camps, air bases and other installations are also sprayed in order to wipe out concealing vegetation and give the defenders a clear field of fire. Areas along the demilitarized zone and the "Ho Chi Minh Trail" in neighboring Laos are also sprayed to help expose infiltrators to bombardment. Rice and other crops that might provide food for the Viet Cong are also attacked, but because of the political implications, each such mission must receive the approval of the American ambassador to South Vietnam. Peasants who lose their crops through the operations of Ranch Hand are supposed to be reimbursed by the American government. But since the money is often distributed by corrupt South Vietnamese provincial chiefs, the peasants are rarely paid in full.

Major Ralph Dresser, USAF, commanding the Ranch Hand operation, declared in an interview in 1966: "We are the most hated outfit in Vietnam. Nobody likes to see the trees and the crops killed. But we're in a war, and Ranch Hand is helping to win it. The Ranch Hand mission is effective and necessary."

The 2-4D chemical defoliant kills plant life by overstimulating growth. The plants literally grow themselves to death. It takes

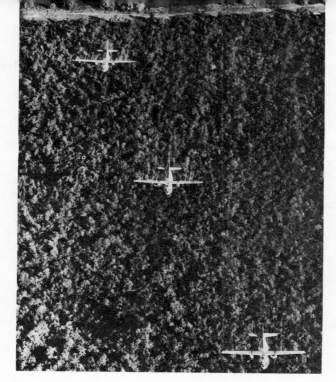

Yankee know-how at work defoliating South Vietnam.

"Only you can prevent forests . . ."

about four days for sprayed leaves to start turning brown and dying. A tree will die in about five or six weeks.

The motto of Operation Ranch Hand, placed above the door of the pilots' ready-room at Tan Son Nhut, reads: ONLY YOU CAN PREVENT FORESTS.

Epilogue

THE WAR WITHOUT END

> The wicked are wicked, no doubt, and they go
> astray and they fall, and they come by their
> deserts; but who can tell the mischief which the
> very virtuous do?
> —WILLIAM MAKEPEACE THACKERAY

THE NIGHTMARE deepened and would not go away. By 1968 more than half a million American soldiers had been sent to fight in the jungles and rice paddies of South Vietnam; more than 40,000 of them would die, many more of them suffer permanently crippling wounds. The direct cost of the war, the cost of supplies and the maintenance of massive air and naval forces and bases consumed an ever larger share of the American military budget: more than fifteen billion dollars per year. And of course the indirect cost in overall military spending increased proportionately. The cost to American relations with the rest of the world, while not so immediately apparent, was hardly less grave.

With the end of the Khrushchev era in Soviet Russia and the assumption of power by the new "managers," Kosygin and Brezhnev, it seemed that the time might be ripe for an easing of the tensions between the United States and the Soviet Union that had produced the Cold War. Changes in Soviet society, signalized by the emergence of a class of "organization men," seemingly uninterested in foreign adventures, as leaders of that society, appeared to lend support to that hope. But the American involvement in Vietnam forestalled all real progress. The Soviet Union had to support the government of North Vietnam and, indirectly, the National Liberation Front in the south, not only because these were Communist entities, but because as Soviet-Chinese relations worsened, Moscow found itself in open competition with Peking for leadership of the Communist world. Not to support North Vietnam and the National Liberation Front would be to abdicate Russian influence in Asia, and perhaps in other areas of the world. The Russians, too, could persuasively develop a "domino theory" to justify their support for Ho Chi Minh's cause.

And if the ongoing battle in South Vietnam and the skies over North Vietnam prevented any meaningful easing of tensions between the United States and Russia, it kept American relations with Red China at the boiling point. Although there was little evidence of direct Chinese intervention in the fighting, Mao Tse-tung had dispatched 40,000 Chinese engineers to North Vietnam —and the largest part of North Vietnam's supplies, both military and economic, came from Red China. The danger of an important clash between Chinese and American forces, intentional or otherwise, could not be dismissed as long as the war went on. And since the United States had taken pains to warn the Chinese that any Korea-style intervention would lead to American bombardment (possibly nuclear) of the Chinese mainland, the potentialities of a third world war developing in Southeast Asia were always clear and present. The United States, faithful to its policy of "containing" the presumed aggressive power of Red China, was bringing overwhelming technical power to bear to control the Asian rimlands. But beyond the rim of that huge continent lay millions of square miles and billions of people beyond American influence. As for Mao Tse-tung's government, it could only look on the continuing American war effort in Vietnam much as an American government might look on a Russian war effort to support a Communist regime in, say, Mexico.

And as the struggle in Vietnam proceeded, American relations with her own allies deteriorated. The governments of Britain, France, West Germany, Japan and others of the "free world" bloc became increasingly alarmed as the United States sank deeper and deeper into the Vietnam quagmire. They worried that American commitments in Southeast Asia might cause the United States to reduce or withdraw its forces from western Europe or the Mediterranean or other strategic areas; they worried that the continuing confrontation in the Far East might lead to the world-annihilating catastrophe of a third world war; they worried because the American "obsession" with Vietnam seemed to indicate a lack of maturity and balance in the leadership of their most powerful ally.

Of perhaps equal significance, the *people* of the "free world" bloc nations as well as the people of the unaligned "third world" nations grew increasingly fearful, increasingly disgusted, increasingly alarmed at American actions in Vietnam. International "congresses" composed of private citizens were held in Stockholm and elsewhere to discuss alleged American "war crimes" in Vietnam; distinguished intellectuals, as for example Britain's Lord Bertrand Russell and France's Jean-Paul Sartre, put themselves at the head of massive bodies of their fellow-citizens to criticize American policy and motives. Throughout the world it was felt, even by those who did not delve deeply into political or strategic pros and cons, that the war in Vietnam was a case of a hugely powerful nation crushing a small, primitive and underdeveloped people; the fact that the powerful nation was "white" (a view ironically interpreted by millions of black Americans who knew that more than fifteen percent of American fighting men in Vietnam were not white) and the small nation was oriental only aggravated public feeling.

But perhaps the highest cost the United States had to pay for the ongoing agony in Vietnam was to be found at home. At a time of social and racial unrest throughout the nation, the bitter burden of the Vietnam War provided a focus of discontent, divided the country as no other issue had divided it since the Civil War. The issue of war or peace, of victory or defeat, of escalation or withdrawal in Vietnam produced student riots and police counterriots, sit-ins, be-ins, teach-ins and passive resistance, bombings of federal buildings, defiance of federal law, marches, demonstrations, and, perhaps most significant of all, a growing distrust on the part of a large number of Americans of their own government. The jargon phrase "credibility gap" came into use as another way of accusing government officials, including Presidents, of outright lying in their promises and statements about Vietnam. The views, arguments and positions of both sides to this bitter domestic quarrel will be examined later. Here it is only necessary to note the terrible legacy of mutual suspicion, distrust and outright hate that divided Americans as the "endless war" dragged on.

For the South Vietnamese, America's massive intervention brought no comfort. The series of plots and counterplots through which a kaleidescope of military men attempted to rule in Saigon came to an end, temporarily at least, when General Ky, with American support, established himself as head of the government in 1966. Two years later, General Ky's dedication to democratic rule being something less than satisfactory in American eyes, he was replaced as head of state by Nguyen Van Thieu, a civilian "elected" president of South Vietnam (with General Ky as vice-president) through highly questionable manipulation of the South Vietnamese ballot. The facts that the government of South Vietnam continued to suppress all political dissent, that the Vietnamese parliament remained a "rubber stamp" legislature, that the vast masses of the South Vietnamese people remained, at best, indifferent to the authorities in Saigon, were underscored by a brutally suppressed Buddhist uprising in 1966 and by the continuing success with which the Viet Cong maintained itself as the "fish" in Vietnamese waters.

And the land and people of South Vietnam paid a terrible price for the all-out war that ravaged their country. Growing out of the earlier concept of strategic hamlets, the idea that the best way to combat guerrillas was to deny them access to the people led to the concept of "free fire zones." Since it was all but impossible to distinguish Viet Cong adherents from the mass of the population, the policy was established of treating "all those not actively with us" as enemies. Vietnamese peasants who did not withdraw from their ancestral villages and fields on command, who were caught out after curfew hours, who were found in zones suspected of harboring Viet Cong detachments—all these, irrespective of sex or age, became fair targets for the overwhelming firepower at the

THE WAR WITHOUT END

disposal of American troops. Entire sections of the country were declared "free fire zones" in which American and South Vietnamese troops might shoot, shell, burn or bomb at will. And since guerrilla tactics were to "hit and run," the United States high command in Saigon adopted the policy of estimating success on the basis of "body counts." Thus an American platoon, company or battalion commander was required to submit a "body count" of enemy dead after each engagement—the number of dead reported being the measure of "victory." This placed pressure on lower-echelon officers to produce a high "kill rate," without paying too much attention to questions of political allegiance. All who were killed were reported as "enemy" dead—and soon all who inhabited areas in which fighting took place were assumed to be "enemy." Hundreds of thousands of South Vietnamese perished as a result of these policies; thousands of villages were wiped out; thousands of square miles of land were devastated.

There is no doubt that American intervention certainly delayed and, temporarily at least, defeated the Viet Cong drive that threatened to engulf South Vietnam in 1964. But there is equally no doubt that although the Viet Cong had been driven from large areas of the country, the membership, morale and influence of the National Liberation Front had not seriously been affected. To underscore that fact, the Viet Cong, early in 1968, during the Vietnamese religious holiday season of *Tet*, undertook a major offensive combined with a local uprising that drove American and South Vietnamese forces from the large city of Hué—a defeat that opened the eyes of the American public to the fact that the United States was not winning the war in Vietnam, despite statements by American military and government leaders to the contrary.

The American escalation of the fighting brought ruin to the cities, towns, fields, transportation systems and factories of North Vietnam. In a sense it paralyzed the social and political revolution undertaken by Ho Chi Minh and his associates by crippling that revolution's economic base. North Vietnam was not a Communist society within the classical Marxist meaning of the word. Rather it was an embattled nation in which the state owned most major enterprises; in which only one political party, the Communist Party, ruled; in which questions of individual freedom were hardly relevant to the overriding question of national survival.

And it was this question of national survival that forced the Hanoi government into greater and greater dependence on the ancient Vietnamese enemy, China. It was all very well for Ho Chi Minh to attempt to maintain his neutrality in the dangerous disputes between Russia and China—Peking was close at hand, Moscow far away. Chinese munitions, weapons and technicians were immediately available, just across the northern border; Russian supplies were harder to receive—most had to travel across China to reach North Vietnam. Furthermore, although the Russians were prepared to install defensive weapons systems (notably the SAM ground-to-air missiles), they appeared to be less than enthusiastic about supporting the ongoing war against the South Vietnamese government and its American ally. Russia, worried about the hazards of nuclear war with the United States, was not anxious to enter situations that might produce a "showdown" between the two world superpowers. China, on the other hand, discounted both the possibility and the potential consequences of nuclear war; in placing itself at the head of the worldwide "national liberation" movement it appeared to be willing to run more risks than the Soviet Union. Perhaps the hardest task faced by Ho Chi Minh after 1966 was to maintain his relative independence from China despite North Vietnam's increasing reliance on Chinese military support.

War, nationalization, deprivation, accommodation with an old enemy—these were not popular policies with all North Vietnamese, yet they were policies Ho was able to pursue, in part at least, simply through the devotion he had earned from his own people. The nature of that devotion was captured in a report printed by the conservative French newspaper Le Monde on September 3, 1966. Le Monde's correspondent in Hanoi was reporting on the annual celebration of North Vietnamese independence on September 2:

"Everyone in the hall seemed to jump for joy when Ho Chi Minh appeared, a frail-looking figure with his narrow, bright-yellow tunic, his samaras (sandals tied with straps) made from an automobile tire, his diaphanous skin and his cheerful face.

President Ho Chi Minh was showing himself in public for the first time that year. . . .

". . . The ceremony began in Russian style, with flowers being presented to the leaders by Pioneers wearing red scarves; it ended in Vietnamese style, in an atmosphere like that of a family gathering. . . .

"Gradually the character of the meeting changed: from a political gathering it turned into 'Grandfather's Day.' M. Ho Chi Minh smoothed down his white beard and addressed the audience, seeking and finding opportunities to make contact with them. 'The front rows,' he said in an atmosphere of collective worship, 'did not sing very loud. . . .' "

Ho Chi Minh died in September 1969. His death, however, appeared to make almost no difference to the dedication and tenacity with which his people continued to pursue their aims, a fact which may be his most fitting monument.

And the war seemed endless . . .

President Lyndon Johnson's political career, perhaps his place in history, was a casualty of the war.

The Democratic Party, shattered at the Chicago convention of 1968 over the issue of war or peace in Vietnam, may well prove to have been a casualty of the war.

President Richard Nixon's ability to unite and lead a divided nation may yet prove to be a casualty of the war.

The reputation of the United States Army, tainted by the breath of torture and massacre, has surely become a casualty of the war.

The confidence of an entire generation of Americans in some of the basic tenets and structures of American society has been a casualty of the war.

It was the war that would not go away, the war from which there seemed no normal escape. Yet it was the war that many Americans found reason to support. These reasons were perhaps best summarized in a speech made on the floor of the United States Senate by Senator Thomas J. Dodd as long ago as February 23, 1965:

"To me the reasons for our presence in Vietnam are so crystal clear that I find it difficult to comprehend the confusion which now appears to exist on this subject.

"We are in Vietnam because our own security and the security of the entire free world demand that a firm line be drawn against further advances of Communist imperialism—in Asia, in Africa, in Latin America, and in Europe.

"We are in Vietnam because it is our national interest to assist every nation, large and small, which is seeking to defend itself against Communist subversion, infiltration, and aggression. There is nothing new about this policy; it is a policy, in fact, to which every administration has adhered since the proclamation of the Truman Doctrine.

"We are in Vietnam because our assistance was invited by the legitimate government of that country.

"We are in Vietnam because, as the distinguished majority leader, the Senator from Montana [Mr. Mansfield], pointed out in his 1963 report, Chinese Communist hostility to the United States 'threatens the whole structure of our own security in the Pacific.'

"We are in Vietnam not merely to help the fourteen million South Vietnamese defend themselves against communism, but because what is at stake is the independence and freedom of 240 million people in Southeast Asia and the future of freedom throughout the western Pacific.

"These are the reasons why we are in Vietnam. There is nothing new about them and nothing very complex. They have never been obscure. They have never been concealed. I cannot, for the life of me, see why people fail to understand them."

Four months later, replying to Senator Dodd's speech, Senator William J. Fulbright spoke the words that were then and have remained the central conviction of those very many Americans who are opposed to American intervention in Southeast Asia:

"The most striking characteristic of a great nation is not the mere possession of power but the wisdom and restraint and largeness of view with which that power is exercised. A great nation is one which is capable of looking beyond its own view of the world,

or recognizing that, however convinced it may be of the benefi-
cence of its own role and aims, other nations may be equally
persuaded of their benevolence and good intent. It is a mark of
both greatness and maturity when a nation like the United States,
without abandoning its convictions and commitments, is capable
at the same time of acknowledging that there may be some merit
and even good intent in the views and aims of its adversaries. . . .

"In the postwar era it has been demonstrated repeatedly that
nationalism is a stronger force than communism and that the association of the two, which has created so many difficulties for the
United States, is neither inevitable nor natural. In the past it has
come about when, for one reason or another, the West has set
itself in opposition to the national aspirations of the emerging
peoples. It is to be hoped that in the future the United States will
leave no country in doubt as to its friendship and support for
legitimate national aspirations. If we do this, I do not think that
we will soon find ourselves in another conflict like the one in
Vietnam."

And it is precisely here that history, which relies on perspective,
time and (the revelations of the Pentagon Study notwithstand-
ing) the use of documentation from many sources which may not
be available for decades, must end: beyond this point too much
remains stormy controversy and bitter debate. Yet, if it is as yet
impossible for an American historian to bring conclusions to bear
on still-inconclusive events, it could be worthwhile to imagine
how a North Vietnamese historian might attempt to conclude *his*
brief study of the long agony that has enveloped his nation. Perhaps, taking a long-range view of matters, he might conclude that
the United States, by its intervention in Vietnam, had brought
a finally decisive influence to bear *not* upon his nation, but rather
upon itself. He might point out that the years following 1965
were *not* the years in which Vietnam bowed before the awesome
power of America; on the contrary, they were the years in which
the Vietnamese Revolution finally reached the United States.

Bibliography

Aptheker, Herbert. *Mission to Hanoi.* New York: 1966.
Bator, Victor. *Viet-Nam: A Diplomatic Tragedy.* Dobbs Ferry, N.Y.: 1965.
Bouscaren, Anthony D. *The Last of the Mandarins: Diem of Viet-Nam.* Pittsburgh: 1965.
Browne, Malcolm. *The New Face of War.* Indianapolis, Ind.: 1965.
Burchett, Wilfred G. *The Furtive War.* New York: 1965.
——— *Vietnam: Inside Story of the Guerrilla War.* New York: 1965.
Buttinger, Joseph. *The Smaller Dragon.* New York: 1958.
——— *Vietnam: A Dragon Embattled.* (2 vols.) New York: 1967.
Cameron, James. *Here Is Your Enemy.* New York: 1966.
Clutterbuck, Richard L. *The Long, Long War.* New York: 1966.
Fall, Bernard B. *Hell in a Very Small Place.* Philadelphia: 1967.
——— *The Two Vietnams.* New York: 1967.
——— *Viet-Nam Witness, 1953-1966.* New York: 1966.
——— and Raskin, Marcus G. (Eds.). *The Vietnam Reader.* New York: 1967.
Gettleman, Marvin E. (Ed.). *Viet-Nam: History, Documents, and Opinions on a Major World Crisis.* New York: 1965.
Goodwin, Richard N. *Triumph or Tragedy.* New York: 1966.
Gurtov, Melvin. *The First Vietnam Crisis.* New York: 1967.
Halberstam, David. *The Making of a Quagmire.* New York: 1965.
Hammer, Ellen J. *The Struggle for Indochina.* Stanford, Calif.: 1954.
——— *Vietnam Yesterday and Today.* New York: 1966.
Harvey, Frank. *Air War—Vietnam.* New York: 1967.

Hickey, Gerald C. *Village in Viet-Nam*. New Haven, Conn.: 1964.
Higgins, Marguerite. *Our Vietnam Nightmare*. New York: 1965.
Ho Chi Minh. *Selected Works*. (3 vols.) Hanoi: 1961.
Hoang Van Chi. *From Colonialism to Communism*. New York: 1964.
Lacouture, Jean. *Ho Chi Minh: A Political Biography*. New York: 1968.
———— *Vietnam: Between Two Truces*. New York: 1966.
Lucas, Jim G. *Dateline: Viet Nam*. New York: 1966.
Mao Tse-tung. *On Protracted War*. Peking: 1960.
Mecklin, John. *Mission in Torment*. Garden City, N.Y.: 1965.
Newman, Bernard. *Report on Indo-China*. London: 1953.
Osborne, M. E. *Strategic Hamlets in South Viet-Nam*. Ithaca, N.Y.: 1965.
Pike, Douglas. *Viet Cong*. Cambridge, Mass.: 1966.
Read-Collins, N. *Report on War in Indochina*. London: 1953.
Reischauer, Edwin O. *Beyond Vietnam*. New York: 1967.
Riessen, Rene. *Jungle Mission*. New York: 1957.
Roy, Jules. *The Battle of Dien Bien Phu*. New York: 1965.
Salisbury, Harrison E. *Behind the Lines—Hanoi*. New York: 1967.
Salmon, Malcolm. *Focus on Indo-China*. Hanoi: 1961.
Scigliano, Robert G. *South Vietnam: Nation Under Stress*. Boston: 1963.
Shaplen, Robert. *The Lost Revolution: The U.S. in Vietnam*. New York: 1965.
Starobin, Joseph R. *Viet-Nam Fights for Freedom*. London: 1953.
Tanham, George K. *Communist Revolutionary Warfare*. New York: 1961.
———— et al. *War Without Guns: American Civilians in Rural Vietnam*. New York: 1966.
Thompson, Sir Robert G. *Defeating Communist Insurgency*. New York: 1966.
Trager, Frank N. *Why Viet Nam?* New York: 1966.
Tregaskis, Richard W. *Vietnam Diary*. New York: 1964.
Truong Chinh. *Primer for Revolt*. New York: 1963.
United States Department of Defense. *Aggression from the North*. Washington, D.C.: 1965.
———— *Viet-Nam: The Struggle for Freedom*. Washington, D.C.: 1964.
United States Senate. *The Viet-Nam Hearings*. New York: 1966.
Vo Nguyen Giap. *People's War, People's Army*. New York: 1962.
Warner, Denis. *The Last Confucian*. London: 1964.

Recommended Reading

Browne, Malcolm W. *The New Face of War*. New York: 1965. A realistic, intimate report by a Pulitzer Prize-winning reporter.

Cameron, James. *Here Is Your Enemy*. New York: 1966. An objective, firsthand account of conditions in North Vietnam.

Fall, Bernard B. *The Two Viet-Nams*. New York: 1967. Excellent on the background of Vietnamese leaders and the rise of the Second Vietnam War.

———— and Raskin, Marcus G. *The Vietnam Reader*. New York: 1967. Very good collection of documents, speeches, reports, etc., presenting the several viewpoints on Vietnam.

Hickey, Gerald C. *Village in Viet-Nam*. New Haven, Conn.: 1964. Excellent study of daily life in the Vietnamese countryside.

Lacouture, Jean. *Ho Chi Minh: A Political Biography*. New York: 1968. Perhaps the best available biography in English of Ho Chi Minh.

Salisbury, Harrison E. *Behind the Lines—Hanoi*. New York: 1967. A fascinating close-up of North Vietnam by one of America's most notable journalists.

PHOTO CREDITS

Index

186

Vietminh—*Cont.*

tion Committee, 70–1; against Japan and France, 72–5; control of Indochina, 76–7; negotiations with French, 82–5; agreement reached, 85–8; terrorist war against French, 88–96, 100–2, 110–5; seized French forts near China border, 100–1; war extends into Laos and Cambodia, 101–2, 110–1; U.S. view of, 108; Red Chinese aid to, 110; Dien Bien Phu, 111–5; controlled most of Vietnam, 119; became Democratic Republic of Vietnam, 120; at Geneva Conference (1954), 120–1; provisions in final accords, 121, 123; leaders went underground in South Vietnam, 124, 139, 144–5; persecuted by Diem regime, 126; and religious-political sects, 138–9; murdered village chiefs, 139; veterans create National Liberation Front, 145

Vietnam: geography, 16–7; aspirations for independence, 16, 19; history, 17–24; population, 17, 24; kingdom established, 19; language, 21–2; social structure, 21–6; bureaucracy, 22–4; government structure, 22–6; French colonialism, 34; Franco-Spanish Expeditionary Force, 36; economic development under French, 42; French military conscription of Vietnamese, 42–3; Communist Party formed, 55–6; Ho Chi Minh leads revolution, 56–7; Japanese domination, 67; Democratic Republic planned by Ho, 68; independence movement, 71–2; Vietminh proposal, 74; Democratic Republic founded, 77; Ho Chi Minh wins election, 84; Republic formed by agreement with French, 85; terrorist activities against French, 88–96; government retreats to Tonkin, 90; Geneva Conference (1954), 120–3; elections proposed, 121, 123,

Vietnam—*Cont.*

127–8; population movements, 124; ancient distrust of China, 144; one nation, 144–5; reunification proposed, 165

Vietnam, North: mountains, 17; communism in, 27, 29–30; military dedication, 29–31; French colony of Tonkin, 39; bombed by U.S., 60–1, 161–5; antiaircraft defenses, 60–62; U.S. prisoners of war in, 63; air reconnaissance over, 78; provisions in Geneva accords, 123; breaches of Geneva accords, 126–7; military buildup, 126–8; accepted as permanent government, 136; socialist economy, 142–3; aid from Russia and China, 143–4, 172, 176; supported insurgents in South Vietnam, 145; torpedo boat incident (1964), 160–2; White Paper charges aggression, 163; economy crippled by U.S., 175; Russian missiles, 176; *see also* Tonkin

Vietnam, South: need for liberation, 29–30; agreement to hold elections, 85, 87–8; first U.S. economic advisers in, 108; increase in U.S. aid, 109, 131, 163–4; and Geneva accords, 123–5; economic blockade of North Vietnam, 125; Diem takes over, 126; breaches of Geneva accords, 126–7; covered by SEATO agreement, 129, 130; treatment of prisoners of war, 132–5; accepted as permanent government, 136; religious-political sects, 137–9; class structure of society, 140; counter-insurgency, 144–7; elections not held, 145; "strategic hamlet" concept, 146–7; persecution of Buddhists, 147–50; downfall of Diem government, 150–1; torture of civilians, 152–4; U.S. presence under President Kennedy, 155–7; increased under President Johnson, 158–60; government not supported by people, 158–60;

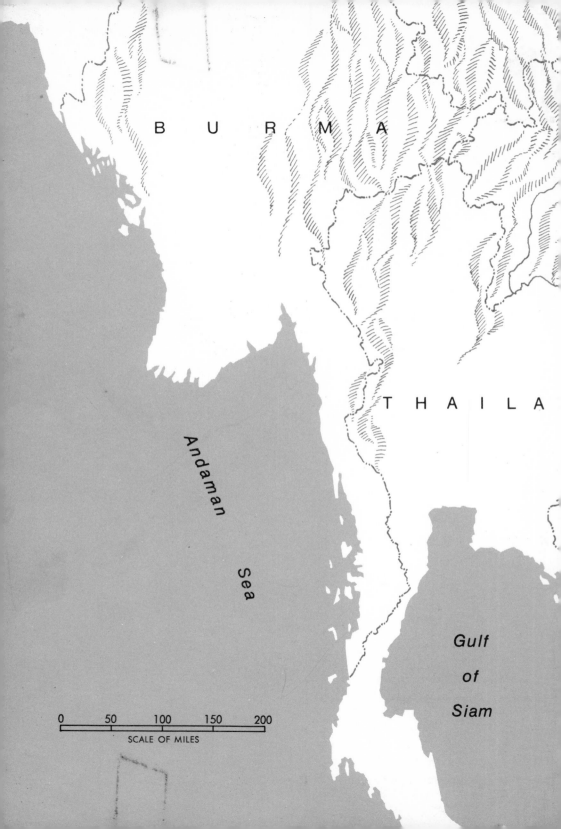